DEUTERONOMY

J. Vernon McGee

THOMAS NELSON PUBLISHERS

Nashville • Atlanta • London • Vancouver

Published in Nashville, Tennessee, by Thomas Nelson, Inc.

Scripture quotations are from the KING JAMES VERSION of the Bible.

Library of Congress Cataloging-in-Publication Data

McGee, J. Vernon (John Vernon), 1904–1988
 [Thru the Bible with J. Vernon McGee]
 Thru the Bible commentary series / J. Vernon McGee.
  p. cm.
 Reprint. Originally published: Thru the Bible with J. Vernon McGee. 1975.
 Includes bibliographical references.
 ISBN 0-7852-1009-1 (TR)
 ISBN 0-7852-1076-8 (NRM)
 1. Bible—Commentaries. I. Title.
BS491.2.M37   1991
220.7′7—dc20   90–41340
                                                      CIP

CONTENTS

DEUTERONOMY

PREFACE

The radio broadcasts of the Thru the Bible Radio five-year program were transcribed, edited, and published first in single-volume paperbacks to accommodate the radio audience.

There has been a minimal amount of further editing for this publication. Therefore, these messages are not the word-for-word recording of the taped messages which went out over the air. The changes were necessary to accommodate a reading audience rather than a listening audience.

These are popular messages, prepared originally for a radio audience. They should not be considered a commentary on the entire Bible in any sense of that term. These messages are devoid of any attempt to present a theological or technical commentary on the Bible. Behind these messages is a great deal of research and study in order to interpret the Bible from a popular rather than from a scholarly (and too-often boring) viewpoint.

We have definitely and deliberately attempted "to put the cookies on the bottom shelf so that the kiddies could get them."

The fact that these messages have been translated into many languages for radio broadcasting and have been received with enthusiasm reveals the need for a simple teaching of the whole Bible for the masses of the world.

I am indebted to many people and to many sources for bringing this volume into existence. I should express my especial thanks to my secretary, Gertrude Cutler, who supervised the editorial work; to Dr. Elliott R. Cole, my associate, who handled all the detailed work with the publishers; and finally, to my wife Ruth for tenaciously encouraging me from the beginning to put my notes and messages into printed form.

Solomon wrote, ". . . of making many books there is no end; and much study is a weariness of the flesh" (Eccl. 12:12). On a sea of books that flood the marketplace, we launch this series of THRU THE BIBLE with the hope that it might draw many to the one Book, *The Bible.*

J. VERNON MCGEE

The Book of
DEUTERONOMY

INTRODUCTION

As we come to the Book of Deuteronomy, I should remind you that this is the last book of the Pentateuch. The first five books in the Bible were written by Moses and they are called the Pentateuch. These books are Genesis, Exodus, Leviticus, Numbers, and Deuteronomy.

The Greek word *deutero* means "two" or "second," and *nomion* is "law." So the title *Deuteronomy* means "the second law." We are not to infer that this is merely a repetition of the Law as it was given to Moses on Mount Sinai. This is more than a recapitulation. It is another illustration of the law of recurrence, as we have already seen in Scripture. The Spirit of God has a way of saying something in an outline form, then coming back and putting an emphasis upon a particular portion of it.

There are four Hebrew titles of Deuteronomy: (1) *Debarim*, meaning "The Words" or "These be the Words," is derived from the opening expression, "These are the words which Moses spake." (2) The *Kith*, or the Fifth of the Law. (3) The Book of Reproofs. (4) The Iteration of the Law.

The theme of Deuteronomy may surprise you. The great theme is *Love and Obey.* You may not have realized that the love of God was mentioned that far back in the Bible, but the word *love* occurs twenty-two times. The Lord Jesus was not attempting to give something that was brand new when He said, "If you love me, keep my commandments." Deuteronomy teaches that obedience is man's response to God's love. This is not the gospel, but the great principle of it is here. And let's understand one thing: the Law is good. Although I emphasize and overemphasize the fact that God cannot save us by Law, that does not imply that the Law is not good. Of course the Law is good. Do you know where the trouble lies? The trouble is with you and me. Therefore God must save us only by His grace.

Moses wrote Deuteronomy. Moses was a man who knew God; he talked with God face to face. The Psalmist says, "He made known his ways unto Moses, his acts unto the children of Israel" (Ps. 103:7). The children of Israel saw the acts of God, but did not know Him. Moses knew His ways. Deuteronomy is the result of this intimate knowledge, plus the experience of forty years in the wilderness.

The section dealing with the death of Moses (Deut. 34:5–12) was probably written by Joshua and belongs to the Book of Joshua. When the Book of Joshua was written, it was placed on the scroll of the Pentateuch, making a Hexateuch.

The authorship of Deuteronomy has been challenged by the critics. The original criticism was that Moses could not have written it because no writing existed in Moses' day. That theory has been soundly refuted, as we now know that writing existed long before Moses' time. Also the critics stated that the purpose of the book was to glorify the priesthood at Jerusalem, yet neither the priesthood nor Jerusalem is even mentioned in the Book of Deuteronomy. It is amazing to see that this Graf-Wellhausen hypothesis, as it is known, which came out of the German universities years ago, is still being taught in many of our seminaries in the United States.

The Book of Deuteronomy was given to the new generation that was unfamiliar with the experiences at Mount Sinai. The new generation had arrived on the east bank of the Jordan River, and it was one month before they would enter the Promised Land. The adults of the generation which had left Egypt were dead, and their bones were bleaching beneath the desert skies because of their unbelief and disobedience. They had broken God's Law—those were sins of commission. They had failed to believe God—those were sins of omission. You see, unbelief is sin. The Law was weak through the flesh. It was the flesh that was wrong, as wrong as it is today. This is the reason God has an altogether different basis on which He saves us.

The new generation, now grown to adulthood, needed to have the Law interpreted for them in the light of thirty-eight years' experience in the wilderness. New problems had arisen which were not covered by the Law specifically. Also God tells His people that they are to teach the Law constantly to their children. By the way, I wonder if this isn't the great neglect in the modern home. We talk about the failure of the school and the failure of the church today, and I agree that both have miserably failed in teaching boys and girls, but the real problem is in the home where instruction should have originated.

Moses gives to this new generation his final instructions from the Lord before he relinquishes his leadership of the nation through death. He reviews the desert experiences, he reemphasizes certain features of the Law, and he reveals their future course in the light of the Palestinian covenant that God had made with him relative to the Land of Promise. We will see in this book that the Mosaic Law was not only given to a people, it was given to a land also.

Finally, Moses teaches them a new song; he blesses the twelve tribes; and then he prepares to die. A requiem to Moses concludes the Book of Deuteronomy.

One Hebrew division of Deuteronomy is very good and follows the generally accepted pattern:

EIGHT ORATIONS

First Oration—1:6—4:40
Second Oration—4:44—26:19
Third Oration—27—28
Fourth Oration—29—30
Fifth Oration—31:1-13
Sixth Oration—32 (Song of Moses)
Seventh Oration—33
Eighth Oration—34

OUTLINE

CHAPTER 1

Moses is reviewing the journeys of the children of Israel and interpreting a great deal of what had taken place. All of that generation is now dead, with the exception of Caleb and Joshua. He is preparing the new generation to enter the land, and rehearsing the experiences of their fathers so that they might profit from them rather than repeat the failures.

These be the words which Moses spake unto all Israel on this side Jordan in the wilderness, in the plain over against the Red sea, between Paran, and Tophel, and Laban, and Hazeroth, and Dizahab [Deut. 1:1].

In that same area I stood on Mount Nebo—I have pictures which I made there—and I actually could see the city of Jerusalem from that elevation. What I saw did not look like a promised land at all. It looked like a total waste, and this reveals what has happened to that land down through the centuries. When Moses looked at it, I think he was seeing a green and a good land. Today it is a desert. It looks like the desert area of California and Arizona.

(There are eleven days' journey from Horeb by the way of mount Seir unto Kadesh-barnea.) [Deut. 1:2].

Mount Sinai is in Horeb. It was a journey of eleven days from Horeb to Kadesh-barnea, which was the entrance point into the Land of Promise. Israel spent thirty-eight years wandering when it should have taken them only eleven days to get into the land. Why? Because of their unbelief. Their marching was turned to wandering, and they became just strangers and pilgrims in that desert. Because they were slow to learn, they wandered for thirty-eight years in that great and terrible wilderness.

We also are slow to learn, friends. I think we would characterize ourselves by saying we have low spiritual I.Q.'s. It seems as if the Lord must burn down the school in order to get some of us out of it!

> **And it came to pass in the fortieth year, in the eleventh month, on the first day of the month, that Moses spake unto the children of Israel, according unto all that the LORD had given him in commandment unto them [Deut. 1:3].**

At the close of their time of wandering, Moses delivers his first oration to them. Obviously his words were first given orally and then were written down later. The critics formerly found fault with this, claiming there was no writing at the time of Moses. Of course, now it has been shown that writing was in existence long before Moses. Moses was the spokesman who gave the oration, yet he makes it clear that this was given him by the Lord.

In reviewing their history and in going over their journeys in detail, Moses mentions his great mistake.

> **And I spake unto you at that time, saying, I am not able to bear you myself alone:**
>
> **How can I myself alone bear your cumbrance, and your burden, and your strife?**
>
> **Take you wise men, and understanding, and known among your tribes, and I will make them rulers over you [Deut. 1:9, 12–13].**

We find the account of this back in Exodus 18. Moses became provoked, burdened, and frustrated. He thought he alone carried the burden of Israel. The Lord permitted him to appoint elders; so a committee of seventy was appointed. This later became the Sanhedrin, the organization which committed Christ to death many years later.

Moses, in his frustration, lost sight of the fact that God was bearing Israel. Moses was God's appointed leader; he didn't need a board or a committee. Moses made a real mistake and he mentions it here. Very few people will mention their mistakes, but Moses does. He says it sounded so good, but it didn't work and it caused a great deal of difficulty.

This same thing can happen in a church. I think one of the worst things that can happen to a church is a board that will not follow the pastor. In that kind of conflict, either the board should go or the pastor should go. If the pastor is standing for the Word of God and is preaching it, then it is the duty of the board to support him. If they don't like the way the pastor parts his hair, they should get out. Unfortunately, usually they stay on, split the church, and try to crucify the preacher.

Do you want to know Moses' estimation of the wilderness they went through?

And when we departed from Horeb, we went through all that great and terrible wilderness, which ye saw by the way of the mountain of the Amorites, as the LORD our God commanded us; and we came to Kadesh-barnea [Deut. 1:19].

I'll take his word for it, because he was there. It was both great and terrible. The wilderness march was no nice daisy trail which they were following.

The second mistake which Moses records was the decision at Kadesh-barnea. This was a mistake of the people. Again, it was the problem of having a board or committee.

And I said unto you, Ye are come unto the mountain of the Amorites, which the LORD our God doth give unto us.

Behold, the LORD thy God hath set the land before thee: go up and possess it, as the LORD God of thy fathers hath said unto thee; fear not, neither be discouraged.

And ye came near unto me every one of you, and said, We will send men before us, and they shall search us out the land, and bring us word again by what way we must go up, and into what cities we shall come.

And the saying pleased me well: and I took twelve men of you, one of a tribe [Deut. 1:20-23].

Here we go again! We must have a board or a committee to go in and search out the land. God had already searched it out! God had said it was a land of milk and honey. Sure, there were giants in the land, but God had said that He would take care of them. The people wanted a board; Moses wanted a board. Look what happened. This was the reason they were turned back into that awful wilderness.

The basic problem is unbelief. God had said it was a good land. The spies looked it over and agreed that it was a good land. But they said there were giants in the land. God had said that He would take care of the giants because He would enable Israel. They did not believe God.

Many times the Christian today finds himself confronted by giants in his life. I'm sure that as a child of God you have found yourself in giant country. Believe me, it is difficult to know how to handle a giant when you are just a pygmy yourself. God has given us the same promise that *He* is able to handle the giants for us. It is wonderful to know that. It is not our circumstances on the outside which are our real problem. It is the circumstance on the inside of us, the unbelief in our hearts, which is the cause of our problems.

Now God makes it clear to them that the whole generation which came up to Kadesh-barnea and turned back in unbelief will die. Only two men of the old generation will be permitted to enter the land. They are Joshua and Caleb.

And the LORD heard the voice of your words, and was wroth, and sware, saying,

Surely there shall not one of these men of this evil generation see that good land, which I sware to give unto your fathers.

Save Caleb the son of Jephunneh; he shall see it, and to him will I give the land that he hath trodden upon, and to his children, because he hath wholly followed the LORD.

Also the LORD was angry with me for your sakes, saying, Thou also shalt not go in thither.

But Joshua the son of Nun, which standeth before thee, he shall go in thither: encourage him: for he shall cause Israel to inherit it [Deut. 1:34–38].

Caleb and Joshua were different from the others. They were spies who believed God and had brought back an accurate report, a good report. The fact of the matter is that Caleb will lay hold of the land that he wanted. We will find later, in the Book of Joshua, that he was a remarkable man. He walked up and down the land, and he claimed the mountain where the giants lived! "This is what I want," he said, and God gave it to him for an inheritance.

By the way, what do you want of God, friend? Are you a parent? Are you a young person starting out in life? What do you want of God? Let me say this: If you think you can sit on the sidelines and get it, you are wrong. There are a great many folk who think they should just sit and pray and pray and pray. I certainly agree that we must pray and live in fellowship with Him, but, my friend, you are going to have to go out there and take it. Did you know that? God said He would give to Caleb the land that he had trodden upon. A great many of us today are not being blessed because we are spending too much time sitting down. That is the wrong place to be if we want the blessing of God. We are to walk. There is a great deal said in the Scriptures about the

Christian's walk and very little said about the Christian's sitting down. We need to lay hold of God's promises.

Joshua is the man who is to become the leader to succeed Moses. Why was he chosen? Well, he is a man of experience, and he is a man who wholly followed God. He and Caleb brought back the good report because they believed God. Faith was the essential thing. They believed God and they were willing to step out in faith. Friend, you don't believe God by just sitting down and claiming great blessings. You have to step out in faith for Him.

> **Moreover your little ones, which ye said should be a prey, and your children, which in that day had no knowledge between good and evil, they shall go in thither, and unto them will I give it, and they shall possess it [Deut. 1:39].**

There are some very important things here that we don't want to miss. First, the age of responsibility is older than we may think it is. Some of these folk who entered the land were teenagers at Kadesh-barnea. We know from Numbers 14:29 that God set the age at 20, and all from twenty years old and upward died in the wilderness.

Something else to note here is that children who die in infancy are saved. How do I know? God did not hold responsible those young folk who had not reached the age of accountability when their elders refused to enter the land. He permitted them to enter the land. You see, the older generation had said they did not want to enter the land because they feared for their children's safety—they were thinking of their children. God made it very clear to them that this was not their real reason. They were insulting God; they were really saying that God didn't care for their children. In effect God says to them, "I do care for your children, and those little ones whom you thought would be in such danger are the very ones who are going to enter the land." Now it is that generation of young folk who have come to the border of the land and are ready to enter the Promised Land. It is to them that Moses is speaking.

> But as for you, turn you, and take your journey into the
> wilderness by the way of the Red sea.
>
> Then ye answered and said unto me, We have sinned
> against the LORD, we will go up and fight, according to
> all that the LORD our God commanded us. And when ye
> had girded on every man his weapons of war, ye were
> ready to go up into the hill [Deut. 1:40–41].

After the children of Israel refuse to go into the land at Kadesh-barnea,
they face a terrible dilemma. They face the wilderness if they turn
back—remember that Moses called it "that great and terrible wilderness." Realizing they have sinned, and realizing they face the wilderness if they turn back, they decide to go into the Promised Land after
all.

> And the LORD said unto me, Say unto them, Go not up,
> neither fight; for I am not among you; lest ye be smitten
> before your enemies [Deut. 1:42].

May I say to you that such a type of fighting is no good. Do you know
why? Because they were out of the will of God. The reason they were
willing to fight at this time was not because they believed God but
because they were afraid. Their motivation was fear, not faith! They
were motivated by fear, not by faith in God.

> So I spake unto you; and ye would not hear, but rebelled
> against the commandment of the LORD, and went pre-
> sumptuously up into the hill [Deut. 1:43].

This was not faith, you see. If they had gone up at the beginning because they believed God, that would have been one thing. This now is
acting presumptuously and is altogether different.

I think there is a very fine distinction between faith and presumption. In the course of my ministry, I have counseled with many people. One man told me, "You know, Brother McGee, I believed God and

I thought He would bless my business. I went into business believing He would bless me, but He didn't. In fact, I went bankrupt." Well, friend, was it faith in God or was it presumption? When we got down to the nitty-gritty, I learned that this man had heard another business man speak at a banquet. His message had been that he had taken as his motto, "God is my partner," and he had been very successful in business. He told about how he had taken God into partnership with him, and God had blessed and prospered him. Obviously, God led that man; I'm confident of that. However, I believe that my friend went home and presumptuously said, "Well, if God will make me prosperous, I'll take Him as my partner in business." God didn't lead him, you see. Believe me, friends, there is a difference between faith and presumption.

And the Amorites, which dwelt in that mountain, came out against you, and chased you, as bees do, and destroyed you in Seir, even unto Hormah.

And ye returned and wept before the LORD; but the LORD would not hearken to your voice, nor give ear unto you.

So ye abode in Kadesh many days, according unto the days that ye abode there [Deut. 1:44–46].

Notice this. They came before the Lord and they shed crocodile tears. They wept, and they repented. Yes, but what kind of a repentance was this? Listen to Paul in 2 Corinthians 7:10: "For godly sorrow worketh repentance to salvation not to be repented of: but the sorrow of the world worketh death."

Did they weep because they disobeyed God? No. They wept because the Amorites had chased them. Their defeat was the reason for their weeping. You know of incidents when a thief is caught, and he begins to shed tears and repent. But wait a minute. What kind of tears are they? Does he weep because he is a thief? No, he weeps because he has been caught. There is a world of difference in that. This is exactly the case with these people.

As a result of all this, they apparently spent a lot of time at Kadesh.

CHAPTER 2

This discourse of Moses gives a continuation of his review of their journeys. After they turned back from Kadesh-barnea, the children of Israel went to Mount Seir.

> **Then we turned, and took our journey into the wilderness by the way of the Red sea, as the LORD spake unto me: and we compassed mount Seir many days [Deut. 2:1].**

I have always thought that the Lord has a sense of humor, and I think we can see it here.

> **And the LORD spake unto me, saying,**
>
> **Ye have compassed this mountain long enough: turn you northward [Deut. 2:2–3].**

You see, they didn't know where to go. All they have been doing is just going around and around Mount Seir. It was sort of a ring-around-the-rosy; round and round they go. Finally God says that He is getting tired of that. He probably said, "Let's quit this round and round business."

I'm afraid many Christians are doing that very same thing. Because they fail to take God at His Word, they are just marking time, and are on a merry-go-round of activity.

GOD'S CARE FOR ESAU

> **And command thou the people, saying, Ye are to pass through the coast of your brethren the children of Esau, which dwell in Seir; and they shall be afraid of you: take ye good heed unto yourselves therefore:**

> Meddle not with them; for I will not give you of their
> land, no, not so much as a footbreadth; because I have
> given mount Seir unto Esau for a possession [Deut.
> 2:4–5].

Here is something else which is important for us to learn. Back in
Genesis 36 we learned that Esau lived in Seir and that Esau is Edom.
Jacob had received the birthright and God gave to him and his descendants the Promised Land. Esau went to Seir, and it is now clear that
God has given that to the people of Esau as their possession. This is in
the country where the rock-hewn city of Petra stands to this day. God
clearly tells Israel that they cannot touch the possession of Esau.

There is a lesson here for the nations today. God has set the bounds
of the nations (Acts 17:26). Most wars are fought because the boundaries of nations are not respected.

Another lesson to learn is that God always keeps His promises.
Even to a people such as the people of Esau, God remains true to His
promise.

> For the Lord thy God hath blessed thee in all the works
> of thy hand: he knoweth thy walking through this great
> wilderness: these forty years the Lord thy God hath
> been with thee; thou hast lacked nothing [Deut. 2:7].

Here is the overall view of their forty years. God knew all their trials
and troubles because God had walked with them all those years.
Moses could honestly say, "Thou hast lacked nothing." How wonderful! It is the same as when David looked back over his life and said,
"The Lord is my shepherd; I shall not want" (Ps. 23:1). How could he
say that? Because he had never wanted! God does not give us the
promise of the luxuries of life, but God provides the necessities of life.
He will do that for you and for me, also.

GOD'S CARE FOR OTHER NATIONS

We have seen how God protected the boundaries of Esau. We find
that He does the same for other nations.

And the LORD said unto me, Distress not the Moabites, neither contend with them in battle: for I will not give thee of their land for a possession; because I have given Ar unto the children of Lot for a possession.

And when thou comest nigh over against the children of Ammon, distress them not, nor meddle with them: for I will not give thee of the land of the children of Ammon any possession; because I have given it unto the children of Lot for a possession [Deut. 2:9, 19].

Israel will face giants in the land, but God encourages them by showing them that for Esau to conquer his land, he had to destroy the giants called Horims (v. 22). For the children of Ammon to possess their land, they had to conquer the giants which were called the Zamzummims (v. 20). We still have giants today. Every now and again we produce people who are 7 and 8 feet tall.

CONQUEST OF TRANS-JORDAN

Rise ye up, take your journey, and pass over the river Arnon: behold, I have given into thine hand Sihon the Amorite, king of Heshbon, and his land: begin to possess it, and contend with him in battle [Deut. 2:24].

Israel passed around Moab and Ammon and did not possess their land. These nations sold them food and water. Now Moses tells of the overtures he made to Sihon, the king of Heshbon.

And I sent messengers out of the wilderness of Kedemoth unto Sihon king of Heshbon with words of peace, saying,

Let me pass through thy land: I will go along by the high way, I will neither turn unto the right hand nor to the left.

> Thou shalt sell me meat for money, that I may eat; and give me water for money, that I may drink: only I will pass through on my feet;
>
> (As the children of Esau which dwell in Seir, and the Moabites which dwell in Ar, did unto me;) until I shall pass over Jordan into the land which the LORD our God giveth us [Deut. 2:26–29].

Instead of allowing Israel to pass through his land, King Sihon came out against them with his armed forces.

> But Sihon king of Heshbon would not let us pass by him: for the LORD thy God hardened his spirit, and made his heart obstinate, that he might deliver him into thy hand, as appeareth this day.
>
> And the LORD said unto me, Behold, I have begun to give Sihon and his land before thee: begin to possess, that thou mayest inherit his land.
>
> Then Sihon came out against us, he and all his people, to fight at Jahaz [Deut. 2:30–32].

God preserved His people from destruction.

> And the LORD our God delivered him before us; and we smote him, and his sons, and all his people [Deut. 2:33].

This land that God allowed Israel to conquer and possess had formerly belonged to the Moabites. The Amorites under King Sihon's leadership had driven out the Moabites from this section of land and had taken over this territory. God permitted him to dispossess the Moabites, but when he led the attack against Israel, he was killed and his forces scattered. His capital was taken and the territory given to Israel. This episode is often referred to as a reminder to Israel of what

God had done for them and became a source of encouragement to them. God is showing them that He is with them and will keep His promises to them.

As you know, the Lord does that for many of us today. He permits us to have a difficult experience, maybe a sad one, to prepare us for life—or to prepare us to be helpful to others.

CHAPTER 3

THEME: Moses reviews Israel's conquest of Bashan

Continuing the rehearsal of Israel's experience in the wilderness, Moses tells of the resistance of another Amorite king and the victory God gave to Israel.

> **Then we turned, and went up the way to Bashan: and Og the king of Bashan came out against us, he and all his people, to battle at Edrei.**
>
> **And the LORD said unto me, Fear him not: for I will deliver him, and all his people, and his land, into thy hand; and thou shalt do unto him as thou didst unto Sihon king of the Amorites, which dwelt at Heshbon [Deut. 3:1–2].**

Notice how the Lord stills their fears.

> **So the LORD our God delivered into our hands Og also, the king of Bashan, and all his people: and we smote him until none was left to him remaining [Deut. 3:3].**

Og was an Amorite king, a man of gigantic stature, whose kingdom seemed invincible.

> **And we took all his cities at that time, there was not a city which we took not from them, threescore cities, all the region of Argob, the kingdom of Og in Bashan [Deut. 3:4].**

Og held sway over sixty separate communities.

> **All these cities were fenced with high walls, gates, and
> bars; beside unwalled towns a great many [Deut. 3:5].**

The fact that Israel was able to conquer this great, well-fortified kingdom was evidence that God fought for Israel. This was a great encouragement to them as they faced giants and the cities "walled up to
heaven" in the Promised Land.

Now let me call your attention to the size of this man Og.

> **For only Og king of Bashan remained of the remnant of
> giants; behold, his bedstead was a bedstead of iron; is it
> not in Rabbath of the children of Ammon? nine cubits
> was the length thereof, and four cubits the breadth of it,
> after the cubit of a man [Deut. 3:11].**

If a cubit is 18 inches, this bed is 13½ feet long! We think today that
the king-size bed is something new. Well, it is not. Here is really a
king-sized bed, friends. Apparently it was preserved as a museum
piece at Rabbath among the Amorites.

POSSESSION OF THE LAND

> **And this land, which we possessed at that time, from
> Aroer, which is by the river Arnon, and half mount Gil-
> ead, and the cities thereof, gave I unto the Reubenites
> and to the Gadites.**
>
> **And the rest of Gilead, and all Bashan, being the king-
> dom of Og, gave I unto the half tribe of Manasseh; all the
> region of Argob, with all Bashan, which was called the
> land of giants [Deut. 3:12–13].**

The conquered kingdom of Og was given to the tribes of Reuben,
Gad, and the half-tribe of Manasseh which chose to stay on the east
side of the Jordan River.

> And I commanded you at that time, saying, The LORD
> your God hath given you this land to possess it: ye shall
> pass over armed before your brethren the children of Is-
> rael, all that are meet for the war [Deut. 3:18].

Moses is reminding them that their being comfortably settled in their
new homes does not free them from the responsibility of helping the
other tribes in their conquest of the land on the west side of the Jordan
River.

> But your wives, and your little ones, and your cattle, (for
> I know that ye have much cattle,) shall abide in your
> cities which I have given you:

> Until the LORD have given rest unto your brethren, as
> well as unto you, and until they also possess the land
> which the LORD your God hath given them beyond Jor-
> dan: and then shall ye return every man unto his pos-
> session, which I have given you [Deut. 3:19–20].

PRAYER OF MOSES

Now Moses recounts his personal experience with the Lord and the
reason he will not be permitted to go into the Promised Land with
them.

> And I besought the LORD at that time, saying,

> O Lord GOD, thou hast begun to shew thy servant thy
> greatness, and thy mighty hand: for what God is there
> in heaven or in earth, that can do according to thy
> works, and according to thy might?

> I pray thee, let me go over, and see the good land that is
> beyond Jordan, that goodly mountain, and Lebanon.

> But the LORD was wroth with me for your sakes, and
> would not hear me: and the LORD said unto me, Let it

suffice thee; speak no more unto me of this matter [Deut. 3:23-26].

Like a good parent, God is true to His Word. In essence He says, "That's enough, Moses. I don't want to hear anymore about it."

Get thee up into the top of Pisgah, and lift up thine eyes westward, and northward, and southward, and eastward, and behold it with thine eyes: for thou shalt not go over this Jordan [Deut. 3:27].

Our hearts go out to this man Moses as he begs the Lord to let him enter the land which has been his goal for forty years. What a lesson this is for us, friends. Though we repent of our sin, we will have to take the consequences of it in this life whether we like it or not.

But charge Joshua, and encourage him, and strengthen him: for he shall go over before this people, and he shall cause them to inherit the land which thou shalt see [Deut. 3:28].

Moses is making it clear to this new generation that stands ready to enter the Promised Land that Joshua is the man the Lord has chosen to be their leader.

CHAPTER 4

THEME: Moses admonishes Israel's new generation

This chapter concludes Moses' review of Israel's wilderness journey. They have come up the east bank of the Jordan River and are near Mount Nebo as Moses gives his final instructions to the people. Only two of the people who made the entire journey stand there—Joshua and Caleb. Most of the people are buried out there in the wilderness, or their bones are bleaching under the desert sun. The new generation is ready now to go into the Promised Land, but before they enter, Moses reviews the wilderness experiences and pleads with them to obey God who loves them.

MOSES PLEADS WITH THEM TO OBEY GOD

Now therefore hearken, O Israel, unto the statutes and unto the judgments, which I teach you, for to do them, that ye may live, and go in and possess the land which the Lord God of your fathers giveth you.

Ye shall not add unto the word which I command you, neither shall ye diminish aught from it, that ye may keep the commandments of the Lord your God which I command you [Deut. 4:1–2].

They are to *do* the Word of God—not only to hear it, but do it. Notice that they were not to add to the Law, neither were they to take away from the Law. They were to obey it as God gave it.

If Israel had kept the Law, what a blessing it would have been. But we find here a demonstration in history of a people who were given the Law under favorable circumstances but who could not keep it. No flesh will be justified before God by the Law. Why not? Is it because God is arbitrary? No, it is because the flesh is radically wrong. That is the problem.

As I have already indicated, this book emphasizes two great themes: love and obedience. Maybe you never realized that love is a great theme of the Old Testament, but it is. Here, in this fourth chapter, Moses is pleading with this new generation, and he is giving to them reasons why they are to obey God.

1. God wants to preserve and prosper Israel.

This first verse tells us that they are to obey the Lord and hearken to His statutes and judgments "that ye may live, and go in and possess the land." Obedience to God is the only basis on which He can bless them. He desires their obedience because it is His desire to bless them.

2. Israel's obedience would show their gratitude to God.

Behold, I have taught you statutes and judgments. . . .

Keep therefore and do them. . . .

For what nation is there so great, who hath God so nigh unto them, as the LORD our God is in all things that we call upon him for?

And what nation is there so great, that hath statutes and judgments so righteous as all this law, which I set before you this day? [Deut. 4:5–8].

God had so marvelously blessed them that they are to show their gratitude through obedience.

3. God's love should prompt their obedience.

And because he loved thy fathers, therefore he chose their seed after them, and brought thee out in his sight with his mighty power out of Egypt [Deut. 4:37].

This is the first time in the Bible that God tells anybody that He loves them. God has *demonstrated* that He loves man from the very first of Genesis, but, up to this point, He hasn't said anything about it. This is the first time He mentions it. He gives this as His motive for what He has done. He has already delivered them out of the land of Egypt, and He is going to do greater and mightier things for them. The basis of it all, the motive for it all, is that God loves them.

This is something which every person today needs to recognize. I don't care who you are, God loves you! You may not always *experience* the love of God. Our sins put up an umbrella between God and us. In spite of our sin, God loves you and He loves me. He has demonstrated that love at the Cross of Christ. When we receive Christ as Savior, we can experience the love of God.

4. They are to obey God because they belong to God.

"Ye are the children of the Lord your God: ye shall not cut yourselves, nor make any baldness between your eyes for the dead" [Deut. 14:1].

Obedience to God is the first law of life, friends. Man has a natural, innate hatred of God. Man doesn't want to obey God; in fact, he is very much opposed to God. All the way through the Word of God we find that there is a resistance on the part of man against God. We find that in man even today.

I am rejoicing in something I heard recently. After I preached in a little church, a lady came up to me and said, "I was saved listening to your program, but I have never been able to get my husband into a church. I have never been able to get him interested, and he has always resisted. Now he is beginning to listen to your program, and it is the only thing he will listen to." If the Word of God won't break down the resistance of a man, nothing else will do it.

If Israel had only kept God's Law! What a blessing would have come to them!

RESULTS OF OBEDIENCE AND OF DISOBEDIENCE

Your eyes have seen what the Lord did because of Baalpeor: for all the men that followed Baal-peor, the Lord thy God hath destroyed them from among you.

But ye that did cleave unto the Lord your God are alive every one of you this day [Deut. 4:3–4].

He is referring to the time when Balaam was called upon to curse Israel, and he could not do it. The fact of the matter is he could pronounce only blessings. But he did make a suggestion to the king of Moab that since he could not curse Israel, the king should let his people go down and intermingle and intermarry with the children of Israel. This would introduce false worship among them which would bring God's judgment down on them. This is exactly what happened, as we saw in chapter 25 of Numbers.

This was to be an example to this new generation. It is to be an example to us also.

There is a reward for obedience. Those who did cleave to the Lord were kept alive and would enter the land. God reminds them again that obedience brings with it a blessing.

> **Behold, I have taught you statutes and judgments, even as the** LORD **my God commanded me, that ye should do so in the land whither ye go to possess it [Deut. 4:5].**

Obedience would bring the blessing of God. They would go into the land to possess it. And their obedience was to serve yet another purpose:

> **Keep therefore and do them; for this is your wisdom and your understanding in the sight of the nations, which shall hear all these statutes, and say, Surely this great nation is a wise and understanding people [Deut. 4:6].**

Israel was to be a witness to all the world. Israel was to witness to the world in the opposite way from the way the church is to witness to the world. We are told "Go ye into all the world, and preach the gospel . . ." (Mark 16:15). That command is given to every believer. Every believer in Christ should have some part in getting the Word of God out to the ends of the earth. Now, very frankly, the nation Israel was never asked to go as missionaries. They were to invite, "Come, let us go up to the house of the Lord." Their obedience, their faithfulness to God, would cause the other nations to hear these statutes and to notice that God's blessing made Israel a great nation. Then what would they do? What did the Queen of Sheba do? She came from the ends of the earth. There were no jet planes at that time. She made a long, arduous, hard trip. If a woman would come that distance under such circumstances, don't you think some men would come to see? And they did. That was the way Israel witnessed to the world. If they would obey, God would bless them, and they would be a witness to all nations. If they would not obey, and if they would turn from the Lord, then God would bring judgment upon them.

Only take heed to thyself, and keep thy soul diligently, lest thou forget the things which thine eyes have seen, and lest they depart from thy heart all the days of thy life: but teach them thy sons, and thy sons' sons [Deut. 4:9].

God gave to the nation Israel the great burden of a teaching ministry. They were to obey God, and they were to teach these things to their children and to their grandchildren.

The greatest undertaking of any nation is the education of the young. Probably the greatest failure of any nation is the failure in education. Look at America today and see the dismal failure we are making in this matter of education. Now I am not blaming the colleges and the schools. Do you know where the problem lies? It is right in the home. God tells these people, "I want you to teach your children and your grandchildren." The failure to teach is the failure of Mom and Dad in the home. This was the great responsibility which God placed upon every father and mother in Israel. Friend, if you are going to bring a child into this world, you are responsible for that child. Our problem today is not foreign affairs or national economy; our problem is the home. God will hold divorced and preoccupied parents responsible for the vagrants of the world today who never knew the instruction and the love and the concern and the communication from parents. What a responsibility parenthood is! God makes this very clear to Israel. When that nation failed, it failed in the home, and God judged it.

And the LORD spake unto you out of the midst of the fire: ye heard the voice of the words, but saw no similitude: only ye heard a voice [Deut. 4:12].

The Lord Jesus stated it very clearly: "God is a Spirit: and they that worship him must worship him in spirit and in truth" (John 4:24). People were never to have any likeness of God whatsoever. The Lord Jesus became a man, but the Bible does not give us any physical description of Him. Now you will probably think I am picayunish, if you haven't already come to that conclusion, but I do not believe in pictures of Jesus. I know that many lovely people feel that a picture of Jesus helps them to worship Him. Let me tell you what was said by an old Scottish commentator: "Men never paint a picture of Jesus until they have lost the presence of Him in their hearts." We need Him in our hearts today, not in color on a canvas. These are tremendous and eternal truths which God is giving us in this chapter. The instructions which were given to Israel in that day are great principles for us to carry over for ourselves today, because truth is eternal.

For the LORD thy God is a consuming fire, even a jealous God.

When thou shalt beget children, and children's children, and ye shall have remained long in the land, and shall corrupt yourselves, and make a graven image, or the likeness of any thing, and shall do evil in the sight of the LORD thy God, to provoke him to anger:

I call heaven and earth to witness against you this day, that ye shall soon utterly perish from off the land whereunto ye go over Jordan to possess it; ye shall not prolong your days upon it, but shall utterly be destroyed.

> And the LORD shall scatter you among the nations, and
> ye shall be left few in number among the heathen,
> whither the LORD shall lead you [Deut. 4:24–27].

That nation is still a witness to the world today, a witness in their disobedience. They are scattered over the world today. Why? Because they did the thing God forbade them to do. I know someone will point out that they are back in the land and they are a nation now. Yes, but they are in trouble, aren't they? When God brings them back into that land as He predicted, they won't be having the trouble they are having today. The nation of Israel is still under the judgment of God today because it has turned its back upon God. Judgment will come upon any nation which rejects Him. This is a tremendous lesson for us today.

> When thou art in tribulation, and all these things are
> come upon thee, even in the latter days, if thou turn to
> the LORD thy God, and shalt be obedient unto his voice
> [Deut. 4:30].

This is the first mention of the Great Tribulation which is ultimately coming. "In the latter days" is a technical term in the Old Testament which refers to the Great Tribulation period. God sets up a condition: "If thou turn to the LORD thy God, and shalt be obedient unto His voice."

> (For the LORD thy God is a merciful God;) he will not
> forsake thee, neither destroy thee, nor forget the cove-
> nant of thy fathers which he sware unto them [Deut.
> 4:31].

Will the Lord scatter them because He is a big bully or because He is being harsh? No, listen. God is merciful. "He will not forsake thee, neither destroy thee." The reason Israel has not been consumed is because God is merciful.

That is the same reason you and I have not been consumed. If you are saved, it is not because you are nice and sweet; it is because of the mercy of God. He is merciful to us as well as to Israel.

Moses goes on to show them the evidence of God's great mercy to them.

> **Did ever people hear the voice of God speaking out of the midst of the fire, as thou hast heard, and live?**

> **Or hath God assayed to go and take him a nation from the midst of another nation, by temptations, by signs, and by wonders, and by war, and by a mighty hand, and by a stretched out arm, and by great terrors, according to all that the LORD your God did for you in Egypt before your eyes? [Deut. 4:33–34].**

God did all these things before the very eyes of their fathers. God does not want them to forget that. God has been gracious to them, and He wants them to remember it.

> **And because he loved thy fathers, therefore he chose their seed after them, and brought thee out in his sight with his mighty power out of Egypt [Deut. 4:37].**

God did it because He loved them. That is the explanation. There was no good in them, but there was good in God.

God loves us today. But He does not save us by love; He saves us by grace. He couldn't just open the back door of heaven and slip us in. He couldn't be righteous and do that. A sacrifice for our sins had to be made. His love sent Christ to die for us, and Christ loved us enough to die so that you and I might have a pardon. The Bible does not say, "God so loved the world, that he saved the world." It says, ". . . God so loved the world, that he *gave* His only begotten Son . . ." (John 3:16). He did this that whoever—it makes no difference who it is— "believeth in Him should not perish, but have everlasting life."

And this is the law which Moses set before the children of Israel:

These are the testimonies, and the statutes, and the judgments, which Moses spake unto the children of Israel, after they came forth out of Egypt [Deut. 4:44–45].

CHAPTER 5

THEME: Moses restates and interprets the Law

This is now the second oration of Moses. It is a restating of the Law, and the emphasis is still on love and obedience. In chapters 5—7 we will find a repetition and interpretation of the Ten Commandments. The generation that had originally heard the Law at Mount Sinai is now dead—their bones are bleaching out there on the desert. This new generation, the Israel that is going into the land, needs to have the Law restated and also interpreted for them. Moses will interpret this in the light of the forty years of experience in the wilderness.

Some of you will say that this is a duplicate of chapter 20 of Exodus. Well, it is almost a duplicate. This shows that the Ten Commandments are important enough to repeat. They are basic, moral laws.

And Moses called all Israel, and said unto them, Hear, O Israel, the statutes and judgments which I speak in your ears this day, that ye may learn them, and keep, and do them [Deut. 5:1].

Here are the four important steps we are to take in relation to the Word of God. The first is to *hear* it. The second is to *learn* it, to become acquainted with what God is saying. The third is to *keep* it. That means to have the Word of God down in your heart. Remember how David spoke of this fact: "Thy word have I hid in mine heart, that I might not sin against thee" (Ps. 119:11). The fourth is to *do* it. Not only should the Word of God be in your head and in your heart, but it should get down there where your feet and hands are.

You hear, as I do, a great many people say that they live by the Ten Commandments, and that's their religion. If you quiz such people, as I have done several times, you will find that what they really mean is they have voted for them—that is, they have heard them and they think they are good. But they certainly are not keeping them and are not obeying them.

The Law actually is like a plumb line to determine the verticality of a crooked wall. The Law is a mirror that is held up to the heart. It is a headlight on a car to show the way into the darkness and to reveal the curves ahead.

God makes it very clear that He is not saving men through the keeping of a moral code. There is nothing wrong with the moral code, the Law, but there is something radically wrong with us. Paul states this in Galatians 2:16: "Knowing that a man is not justified by the works of the law, but by the faith of Jesus Christ, even we have believed in Jesus Christ, that we might be justified by the faith of Christ, and not by the works of the law: for by the works of the law shall no flesh be justified." No one is justified by the Law. Why not? Because no one can do the works of the Law.

"Wherefore then serveth the law? It was added because of transgressions, till the seed should come to whom the promise was made; and it was ordained by angels in the hand of a mediator" (Gal. 3:19). It is logical to ask what the purpose of the Law is. The answer is that it was added because of (or for the sake of) transgressions, until the time when the Seed should come. That is, it was temporary until the Seed should come, and that Seed is Christ. "Wherefore the law was our schoolmaster to bring us unto Christ, that we might be justified by faith. But after that faith is come, we are no longer under a schoolmaster" (Gal. 3:24–25). The Law served as a schoolmaster, a servant to take us by the hand and bring us to the Cross, just as the schoolmaster brought the child to school. The Law brings us to the Cross and says, "Little fellow, you are a sinner and you need a Savior." The purpose of the Law is to show us our need for a Savior. The Law is good, friends; there is no doubt about that. The Law reveals the mind of God. The Law reveals how far short you and I come of the glory of God. The Law reveals that "all have sinned, and come short of the glory of God" (Rom. 3:23). Put this Law down on your life and let it bring you to Christ.

The Lord our God made a covenant with us in Horeb.

The LORD made not this covenant with our fathers, but with us, even us, who are all of us here alive this day [Deut. 5:2-3].

God did not give the Law to them down in Egypt. The Law was not given until they were out in the wilderness at Horeb, which is Mount Sinai. The Law was given to the nation Israel.

The LORD talked with you face to face in the mount out of the midst of the fire,

(I stood between the LORD and you at that time, to shew you the word of the LORD: for ye were afraid by reason of the fire, and went not up into the mount;) saying,

I am the LORD thy God, which brought thee out of the land of Egypt, from the house of bondage [Deut. 5:4-6].

You see, Israel was in a land of idolatry when they lived in Egypt, and Israel lived in an age of idolatry.

Thou shalt have none other gods before me [Deut. 5:7].

Man's first sin was not to become an atheist; his sin was to become a polytheist. He worshiped many gods. For example, at the tower of Babel, men built a ziggurat, a tower. On the top of this they offered sacrifices, apparently to the sun. The sun and the planets were some of the first objects men worshiped when they turned away from God. After the Flood, they certainly were not worshiping thunder and lightning, because they feared them. They worshiped the sun, the creation rather than the Creator. It was for the polytheist that God said, "Thou shalt have none other gods before me." It was not until the time of David that atheism came in. Earlier than that, men were too close to the mooring mast of revelation to be atheists. The revelation of God was still in their memory, and no one was denying the existence of God. In David's day it was the fool who ". . . said in his heart, There is no God" (Ps. 14:1). That word *fool* means "insane." A man who says there is no God is insane or else he is not sincere. This first commandment does not even mention a disbelief in the existence of God, it prohibits the worship of many gods.

> Thou shalt not make thee any graven image, or any likeness of any thing that is in heaven above, or that is in the earth beneath, or that is in the waters beneath the earth:

> Thou shalt not bow down thyself unto them, nor serve them: for I the LORD thy God am a jealous God, visiting the iniquity of the fathers upon the children unto the third and fourth generation of them that hate me,

> And shewing mercy unto thousands of them that love me and keep my commandments [Deut. 5:8–10].

There are only two kinds of people in the world: those who hate God and those who love Him. He goes into detail when He forbids the making of any likeness of anything that could be worshiped. Later on God will say, "Thou shalt love the LORD thy God with all thine heart, and with all thy soul, and with all thy might" [Deut. 6:5]. The Lord Jesus says that this is the greatest commandment. Over against that is the great company of those who hate God even today.

Today many people maintain that they do not worship an idol at all. Yet Paul tells us in Ephesians 5:5 that covetousness is idolatry. Anything that you give yourself to, anything that stands between you and God, becomes your god. You say you have no idol? To some people, their bankbook is their god. Other people worship the golf club. Others may let a child or a grandchild become their idol. The television screen can become your idol. Anything that takes first place in your heart is your idol.

> Thou shalt not take the name of the LORD thy God in vain: for the LORD will not hold him guiltless that taketh his name in vain [Deut. 5:11].

Remember that when Paul shows that all mankind is sinful, he writes, "whose mouth is full of cursing and bitterness" (Rom. 3:14). All you have to do is walk down the street today or be in any public place and you will hear the people with foul mouths. I wonder if there ever have been so many foul-mouthed, dirty-minded folk as there are at the present time. God hates it. God says He will not hold guiltless those who take His name in vain.

A friend of mine challenged me one day and said it wasn't fair to say that man's mouth is full of cursing. I asked him to do a little experiment with me. I suggested we stand on the street corner and hit the first man who came along—hit him in the mouth to see what would come out. My friend, you know what would come out!

The first three commandments are negative; now we come to a positive commandment.

Keep the sabbath day to sanctify it, as the Lord thy God hath commanded thee.

Six days thou shalt labour, and do all thy work:

But the seventh day is the sabbath of the Lord thy God: in it thou shalt not do any work, thou, nor thy son, nor thy daughter, nor thy manservant, nor thy maidservant, nor thine ox, nor thine ass, nor any of thy cattle, nor thy stranger that is within thy gates; that thy manservant and thy maidservant may rest as well as thou.

And remember that thou wast a servant in the land of Egypt, and that the Lord thy God brought thee out thence through a mighty hand and by a stretched out arm: therefore the Lord thy God commanded thee to keep the sabbath day [Deut. 5:12–15].

The very interesting thing is that all of the commandments are repeated in the New Testament with the exception of the commandment about the Sabbath Day. Why? Because the Sabbath was not given to the church. The church has always met on the first day of the week, the day on which Christ rose from the dead. The Sabbath Day has a peculiar relation to the nation Israel. Back in the Book of Exodus, God said, "Speak thou also unto the children of Israel, saying, Verily my sabbaths ye shall keep: for it is a sign between me and you throughout your generations; that ye may know that I am the LORD that doth sanctify you" (Exod. 31:13). The Sabbath was given to Israel.

It is of interest to notice that in Exodus 20 the children of Israel were told to observe the Sabbath because in six days God had created the heavens and the earth. Here in Deuteronomy the Sabbath is to show the peculiar relationship between God and the children of Israel. Why was the Israelite to keep the Sabbath Day? Because he had been a slave in Egypt, and God had brought him out by His great power.

These commandments have been concerned with duty toward God. Now we come to the section concerning duty toward man.

Honour thy father and thy mother, as the LORD thy God hath commanded thee; that thy days may be prolonged, and that it may go well with thee, in the land which the LORD thy God giveth thee [Deut. 5:16].

I believe this commandment is related to duty toward God and man. The father and mother stand in the place of God to the little one who is growing up. The little one looks up to the father and the mother, and that is the way it should be. "My son, hear the instruction of thy father, and forsake not the law of thy mother" (Prov. 1:8). Father and Mother are to stand in the place of God while their children are small.

Now as these people are going into the land promised to them, they are to honor their father and their mother. A nation that does not observe this commandment will not be blessed. This very thing is a great problem in America right now, although I realize full well that not all fathers and mothers are worthy of this respect. God has something to say to parents also: "And, ye fathers, provoke not your children to wrath: but bring them up in the nurture and admonition of the Lord" (Eph. 6:4). Both commandments go together.

Thou shalt not kill [Deut. 5:17].

The word for "kill" here is a very technical word, the Hebrew *ratsach*, and it means to murder. Thou shalt not murder. This is personal. This word has in it the thought of premeditated killing, of anger and of personal grievance. This has nothing to do with war—we will read a little later on that God tells these people to destroy their enemy in the land. This commandment does not apply to a soldier under the orders of war. A young man told me a few years ago that he did not want to go to Vietnam. He said, "I'm not angry at anyone over there. I don't want to go over there to kill." I answered that it was a good thing he was not angry with someone over there. If that were the case, and he went to seek that person out in order to kill him, he would be guilty of murder. We will speak more of this when we talk about our duty to government. The sixth commandment was not intended for a serviceman in combat.

Neither shalt thou commit adultery [Deut. 5:18].

We live in a sex-mad age. Every conceivable product is advertised by sex. It is around us on every hand. God's commandment still stands today. Thou shalt not commit adultery. This is one of the great sins that is pulling our nation down today.

Neither shalt thou steal [Deut. 5:19].

It is true there are many people who can say that they never held up a supermarket or a bank, yet there can be the desire to steal in the heart. Our Lord taught that the very thoughts of our heart are sinful. Hatred in the heart makes one guilty of murder. Lust in the heart makes one guilty of adultery.

Neither shalt thou bear false witness against thy neighbour.

Neither shalt thou desire thy neighbour's wife, neither shalt thou covet thy neighbour's house, his field, or his

> manservant, or his maidservant, his ox, or his ass, or
> any thing that is thy neighbour's [Deut. 5:20-21].

The command against covetousness shows that it is a sin just to feel
an excessive desire for what belongs to another.

Moses rehearses for this younger generation the tremendous experience of receiving the Law directly from God.

> And it came to pass, when ye heard the voice out of the
> midst of the darkness, (for the mountain did burn with
> fire,) that ye came near unto me, even all the heads of
> your tribes, and your elders;
>
> And ye said, Behold, the LORD our God hath shewed us
> his glory and his greatness, and we have heard his voice
> out of the midst of the fire: we have seen this day that
> God doth talk with man, and he liveth.
>
> Now therefore why should we die? for this great fire will
> consume us: if we hear the voice of the LORD our God
> any more, then we shall die.
>
> For who is there of all flesh, that hath heard the voice of
> the living God speaking out of the midst of the fire, as
> we have, and lived? [Deut. 5:23-26].

It was such a terrifying experience that they wanted Moses to get the
message from the Lord and relay it to them:

> Go thou near, and hear all that the LORD our God shall
> say: and speak thou unto us all that the LORD our God
> shall speak unto thee; and we will hear it, and do it
> [Deut. 5:27].

The children of Israel promised to keep the Law, but they did not do it.
Listen now to God's heart-cry for His people:

O that there were such an heart in them, that they would fear me, and keep all my commandments always, that it might be well with them, and with their children for ever! [Deut. 5:29].

The problem was that the nation failed to keep the Law. These people were under favorable conditions, living in the land promised to them—the Law was given for that land as well as that people—but they were unable to keep the Law. That should be a lesson to us. Just as they were unable to keep it so you and I are unable to keep it.

The Law is a mirror held up to us. We are to look in it, and it will reveal to each of us that we are sinners. The mirror in the bathroom will show the smudge spot on the face, but the mirror won't wash off that spot. The Law can show us our sin, but it cannot save us. In no way can the mirror remove the smudge spot. We must come to the basin and wash it away. The Law is the mirror that tells us to start washing. It tells us to come to Christ. It is the blood of Jesus Christ, God's Son, that will wash us and keep on cleansing us from all sin. William Cowper wrote, "There is a fountain filled with blood, drawn from Emmanuel's veins; And sinners plunged beneath that flood lose all their guilty stains."

The important thing is not whether you approve of the Ten Commandments or what you think of them; the important question, my friend is: Have you kept them? If you are honest, you know that you haven't measured up. That means you need a Savior. "Come now, and let us reason together, saith the LORD: though your sins be as scarlet, they shall be as white as snow; though they be red like crimson, they shall be as wool" (Isa. 1:18). When you come to Christ, He forgives you and cleanses you from all unrighteousness. Then you stand spotless before Him.

CHAPTER 6

THEME: Love and obey

As we have noted before, in the Book of Deuteronomy there has been an emphasis on two words: love and obedience—not *law* and obedience, as we may have supposed.

God's love is actually expressed in law. The great principle of law is love. Therefore the principle of the gospel itself is expressed in Deuteronomy. ". . . God so loved the world, that he gave his only begotten Son . . ." (John 3:16).

You and I express our love for God in our obedience. The Lord Jesus put it like this: "If ye love me, keep my commandments" (John 14:15). This is still the acid test today. If we love Him, we will keep His commandments. Salvation is a love affair. "We love him, because he first loved us" (1 John 4:19). The Lord Jesus cited this as the greatest commandment of all: "And thou shalt love the LORD thy God with all thine heart, and with all thy soul, and with all thy might" (Deut. 6:5). Our obedience is the manifestation of our love.

Obedience is the important thing all the way through—it is "*if* they keep these commandments."

Now you may wonder what is new about love in the New Testament if love is in the Old Testament. The difference is that in the New Testament the love of God has been translated into history by the incarnation and death of Christ. "But God commendeth his love toward us, in that, while we were yet sinners, Christ died for us" (Rom. 5:8). He died for us! You see, it is one thing to express love by bringing Israel out of Egypt; it is another thing to die for them. It is one thing to say something from the top of Mount Sinai; it is another thing to come down and take our frail humanity upon Himself, to be made in the likeness of man, and to die on a cross for our sins. I repeat, salvation is a love affair. "Herein is love, not that we loved God, but that he loved us, and sent his Son to be the propitiation for our sins" (1 John 4:10).

We are still in the second oration of Moses. In chapters 5–7, he is giving a repetition and interpretation of the Ten Commandments.

THE GREAT COMMANDMENT

Now these are the commandments, the statutes, and the judgments, which the LORD your God commanded to teach you, that ye might do them in the land whither ye go to possess it:

That thou mightest fear the LORD thy God, to keep all his statutes and his commandments, which I command thee, thou, and thy son, and thy son's son, all the days of thy life; and that thy days may be prolonged [Deut. 6:1–2].

The emphasis is on obedience. There are actually only two classes of people in the world: those who love God and those who hate God. The heart attitude of people is evidenced by their obedience or disobedience. Listen to Deuteronomy 5:29: "O that there were such an heart in them, that they would fear me, and keep all my commandments always, that it might be well with them, and with their children for ever!" Through the prophet Isaiah, God had this to say: "Wherefore the Lord said, Forasmuch as this people draw near me with their mouth, and with their lips do honour me, but have removed their heart far from me, and their fear toward me is taught by the precept of men" (Isa. 29:13). Do you remember how the prophet Samuel rebuked King Saul? "And Samuel said, Hath the LORD as great delight in burnt offerings and sacrifices, as in obeying the voice of the LORD? Behold, to obey is better than sacrifice, and to hearken than the fat of rams" (1 Sam. 15:22). When the Lord Jesus gave His commission to Simon Peter, He asked only one question, "Simon, son of Jonas, lovest thou me?" (John 21:16).

The most wonderful thing in heaven will be to see the Lord Jesus and realize fully that He loves me and that He gave Himself for me.

But the next best thing in heaven is going to be that I will love everybody, and everybody is going to love me. Now that, my friend, is going to make heaven a very wonderful place!

Hear therefore, O Israel, and observe to do it; that it may be well with thee, and that ye may increase mightily, as the LORD God of thy fathers hath promised thee, in the land that floweth with milk and honey [Deut. 6:3].

They had promised to keep all the commandments of the Lord, and yet they fell so short—as we still do today.

Now we come to a statement which is considered by many theologians to be the greatest doctrinal statement in the entire Scripture.

Hear, O Israel: the LORD our God is one LORD [Deut. 6:4].

That is a tremendous statement. "The LORD" is the Hebrew tetragram transliterated YHWH or JHVH, translated in English as Jehovah. "God" is the translation for *Elohim*. *Elohim* is a plural word. Since there is no number given with it, one can assume the number is three. In the Hebrew language a noun is singular, dual, or plural. When it is plural, but no number is given, one can assume it to be three. This is, therefore, a reference to the Trinity. It could be translated, "Hear, O Israel: Jehovah, our Trinity is one Jehovah."

Israel lived in a world of idolatry. The nations were polytheists who worshiped many gods. The message that the nation Israel was to give to the world was the message of the unity of the Godhead, the oneness of the Godhead. Jehovah, our Elohim, is one Jehovah. That is the message for a world given over to idolatry.

Today we live in a world, not so much of idolatry and polytheism, but of atheism. In our age we also are to give the message of the Trinity. God is Father, Son, and Holy Spirit. We are talking about the same Jehovah. He is our Elohim, our Trinity. But He is one Jehovah.

And thou shalt love the LORD thy God with all thine heart, and with all thy soul, and with all thy might [Deut. 6:5].

Our Lord Jesus quotes this as being the greatest commandment of all. "And one of the scribes came, and having heard them reasoning together, and perceiving that he had answered them well, asked him, Which is the first commandment of all? And Jesus answered him, The first of all the commandments is, Hear, O Israel; The LORD our God is one LORD: and thou shalt love the Lord thy God with all thy heart, and with all thy soul, and with all thy mind, and with all thy strength: this is the first commandment. And the second is like, namely this, Thou shalt love thy neighbour as thyself. There is none other commandment greater than these" (Mark 12:28–31).

How do you measure up to this? Many of us would have to confess that we do not measure up to this. We do not love Him with all our mind and heart and soul. I must confess that I do not measure up to this; I wish I could, but I must say with Paul, "Brethren, I count not myself to have apprehended: but this one thing I do, forgetting those things which are behind, and reaching forth unto those things which are before, I press toward the mark for the prize of the high calling of God in Christ Jesus" (Phil. 3:13–14). I do want to say that I love Him. I wish I loved Him more than I do, but He is the object of my affection today. I can truly say that I love Him. That is what He asked Simon Peter. "Do you love Me?" I think He would ask you and me that same question today. To learn to love Him, we must sit at His feet and come to know Him. He is the chiefest among ten thousand. He is the One altogether lovely. He is our God. Peter said, "Lord, to whom shall we go? thou hast the words of eternal life. And we believe and are sure that thou art that Christ, the Son of the living God" (John 6:68–69). He is our Savior. He is our Lord. He is our God. I worship Him. I want to know Him better. What does He mean to you?

"Thou shalt love the Lord thy God with all thine heart, and with all thy soul, and with all thy might." Then the Lord Jesus reached into Leviticus 19:18, and lifted out, "Thou shalt love thy neighbour as thyself." He said the second is like unto the first. Friend, there is no such thing as loving God and hating His people. Remember that when Saul was persecuting the Christians, the Lord Jesus asked him, "Saul, Saul, why persecutest thou me?" (Acts 9:4).

He may be saying the same thing to some Christians today. Although they profess to know and to love the Lord, He asks, "Why are you persecuting Me?" They would protest, "I'm not persecuting You, Lord; I love You!" Then the Lord would answer, "Then why do you criticize Mr. So-and-So so severely? Why are you so opposed to those who are giving out the Word of God today? Why is it that you have become a hindrance instead of a helper?" May I say to you, we must be careful about saying we love Him and then showing our hatred to other believers. It is impossible to talk about loving the Lord while you spend your time trying to destroy the ministry of someone else. That is just blatant, bald, bold hypocrisy.

> **And these words, which I command thee this day, shall be in thine heart [Deut. 6:6].**

You remember that David said, "Thy word have I hid in mine heart, that I might not sin against thee" (Ps. 119:11). That is the place where you and I should have the Word of God today, my friend. It should be in our hearts.

> **And thou shalt teach them diligently unto thy children, and shalt talk of them when thou sittest in thine house, and when thou walkest by the way, and when thou liest down, and when thou risest up.**

> **And thou shalt bind them for a sign upon thine hand, and they shall be as frontlets between thine eyes.**

> **And thou shalt write them upon the posts of thy house, and on thy gates [Deut. 6:7–9].**

Paul says the same thing in Ephesians 6:4: "And, ye fathers, provoke not your children to wrath: but bring them up in the nurture and admonition of the Lord." God holds parents responsible to bring up their children in the discipline and instruction of the Lord. All through the Scriptures there is a great deal said concerning the responsibility of parents. "Train up a child in the way he should go: and when he is old, he will not depart from it" (Prov. 22:6). That does not mean to train him the way you want him to go. It means that God has a way for him to go, and you are to cooperate with God. That means, parent, that you need to stay close to Him!

These words were to be kept before them at all times. We see advertising on billboards and in signs and in neon lights. It is no wonder that America today is turning to liquor and to cigarettes and to drugs. This is what is held before our eyes. It is on the television screen, on the radio, in all the advertising. Young people turn to these things because this is what greets them on every hand. God wants His Word to be taught to His people just like that. It should greet them at every turn. Why? Because the human heart is prone to forget God and His ways.

Then God warns His people that they should not forget Him after they get into the land and experience His blessings. It is a strange thing that when people are blessed, they tend to forget the One who blesses them.

Thou shalt fear the LORD thy God, and serve him, and shalt swear by his name [Deut. 6:13].

Our Lord Jesus used this verse when He was tempted by Satan, as recorded in Matthew 4:10 and in Luke 4:8.

Ye shall not tempt the LORD your God, as ye tempted him in Massah [Deut. 6:16].

This is another verse which our Lord used when He withstood the temptation of Satan, which is quoted in Matthew 4:7 and in Luke 4:12. No wonder that Satan hates the Book of Deuteronomy and levels his attacks against it!

Again God admonishes His people to diligently do His commandments that they might keep the land He is giving to them, and to explain this to their children, also.

And he brought us out from thence, that he might bring us in, to give us the land which he sware unto our fathers.

And the LORD commanded us to do all these statutes, to fear the LORD our God, for our good always, that he might preserve us alive, as it is at this day.

And it shall be our righteousness, if we observe to do all these commandments before the LORD our God, as he hath commanded us [Deut. 6:23–25].

God had brought them *out* of the land of Egypt. His purpose is to bring them *into* the Promised Land. It is just so with our salvation. God has saved us out of death and sin and judgment. He brings us into the body of Christ, into the place of blessing, into fellowship with Himself, and finally, into heaven itself. However, our salvation is still not complete. He was "delivered for our offenses and was raised again for our justification" (Rom. 4:25). He is our righteousness so that we might stand complete before Him. He has brought us out; He intends to bring us in. Because of this we can say today:

I have been saved. We already have eternal life. We already stand before God in all the righteousness and merit of our Savior. "And this is the record, that God hath given to us eternal life, and this life is in his Son. He that hath the Son hath life; and he that hath not the Son of God hath not life" (1 John 5:11–12).

I am being saved. God is working in my life, shaping, guiding, molding me to conform me more and more to His own dear Son. ". . . Work out your own salvation with fear and trembling. For it is God which worketh in you both to will and to do of his good pleasure" (Phil. 2:12–13). This is not working *for* salvation, but the working *out* of salvation in our lives.

I shall be saved. Don't be discouraged with me, because God is not through with me yet. And I won't be discouraged with you, because God is not through with you either. "Beloved, now are we the sons of God, and it doth not yet appear what we shall be: but we know that, when he shall appear, we shall be like him; for we shall see him as he is" (1 John 3:2).

A dear little lady got up in a testimony meeting and said that every Christian should have printed on his back a sign that reads: "This is not the best that the grace of God can do." How true that is! God is not through with any one of us. But "when he shall appear, we shall be like him."

CHAPTER 7

When the Lord thy God shall bring thee into the land whither thou goest to possess it, and hath cast out many nations before thee, the Hittites, and the Girgashites, and the Amorites, and the Canaanites, and the Perizzites, and the Hivites, and the Jebusites, seven nations greater and mightier than thou;

And when the Lord thy God shall deliver them before thee; thou shalt smite them, and utterly destroy them; thou shalt make no covenant with them, nor shew mercy unto them [Deut. 7:1–2].

This is very strong language. Remember that God had said, "Thou shalt not kill." That is a command against personal animosity, personal hatred which leads to murder. The Hebrew word is *ratsach*. Here they are directly commanded to *destroy* these people who were living in the land. It is an altogether different Hebrew word—*charam*, meaning "to devote (to God or destruction)." You may think that is terrible. The liberal today hates the God of the Old Testament. I heard one call God a bully. They don't like the idea that God would actually destroy whole nations. God also says this:

Neither shalt thou make marriages with them; thy daughter thou shalt not give unto his son, nor his daughter shalt thou take unto thy son.

For they will turn away thy son from following me, that they may serve other gods: so will the anger of the Lord be kindled against you, and destroy thee suddenly [Deut. 7:3–4].

Here we have the reason for God's command. These people were eaten up with venereal disease. Had Israel intermarried with them, they would have destroyed the race. Moses didn't understand much about disease germs, but God knows a great deal about them. These people were so polluted and corrupt that God put them out of the land. Not only that, these people were idolatrous, and they would have led Israel into idolatry. So God goes on to tell them that they are to utterly destroy their altars and break down their images. All this polluting influence is to be completely destroyed.

God gives Israel a solemn warning. If they do intermarry and turn to other gods, then God will put them out of the land. And yet, God makes it very clear to Israel that He is the God of love. He gives these commands because He loves them.

> **For thou art an holy people unto the Lord thy God: the Lord thy God hath chosen thee to be a special people unto himself, above all people that are upon the face of the earth.**

> **The Lord did not set his love upon you, nor choose you, because ye were more in number than any people; for ye were the fewest of all people [Deut. 7:6–7].**

Never a great nation numerically, they would not compare to China or India or other great nations of the world.

> **But because the Lord loved you, and because he would keep the oath which he had sworn unto your fathers, hath the Lord brought you out with a mighty hand, and redeemed you out of the house of bondmen, from the hand of Pharaoh king of Egypt [Deut. 7:8].**

You remember that God said in Exodus that He had heard their cry, that distress cry. He responded because He loved them. He delivered them from bondage for that reason. He keeps repeating this.

> Know therefore that the Lord thy God, he is God, the
> faithful God, which keepeth covenant and mercy with
> them that love him and keep his commandments to a
> thousand generations [Deut. 7:9].

What is man's answer to the love of God? It is obedience.

> And repayeth them that hate him to their face, to destroy
> them: he will not be slack to him that hateth him, he
> will repay him to his face.
>
> Thou shalt therefore keep the commandments, and the
> statutes, and the judgments, which I command thee this
> day, to do them [Deut. 7:10–11].

God will bless any people who respond to His love by obedience.

> Wherefore it shall come to pass, if ye hearken to these
> judgments, and keep, and do them, that the Lord thy
> God shall keep unto thee the covenant and the mercy
> which he sware unto thy fathers:
>
> And he will love thee, and bless thee, and multiply thee:
> he will also bless the fruit of thy womb, and the fruit of
> thy land, thy corn, and thy wine, and thine oil, the in-
> crease of thy kine, and the flocks of thy sheep, in the
> land which he sware unto thy fathers to give thee [Deut.
> 7:12–13].

How wonderful it would have been if Israel had believed God!
God encourages them, and He promises them victory—

> Thou shalt not be afraid of them: but shalt well remem-
> ber what the Lord thy God did unto Pharaoh, and unto
> all Egypt [Deut. 7:18].

The faithfulness of God in the past should be an encouragement for
them in the future. Isn't it precisely the same with us?

**Thou shalt not be affrighted at them: for the LORD thy
God is among you, a mighty God and terrible.**

**And the LORD thy God will put out those nations before
thee by little and little: thou mayest not consume them at
once, lest the beasts of the field increase upon thee
[Deut. 7:21–22].**

We see God's wisdom here. He is thinking of their safety, knowing
that if the population were destroyed suddenly, the wild animals
would take over the land.

**But the LORD thy God shall deliver them unto thee, and
shall destroy them with a mighty destruction, until they
be destroyed [Deut. 7:23].**

All these nations were to be put out of the land and utterly destroyed
because of their abominations. Now don't say that God had not been
patient with them. Way back in Genesis 15:16 God had told Abraham
that his descendants would not come back into the land until the
fourth generation "for the iniquity of the Amorites is not yet full." God
gave these people 430 years to see whether they would turn to God
and turn from their sins. Friends, how much more time do you want
God to give them? Do you know any other landlord who will give his
tenant that long a time to pay his rent? God gave them a time of mercy
that lasted for 430 years. Then the cup of iniquity was full, and the
judgment of God fell upon them. So let us not have a false kind of pity
for these nations. Rather, let us learn from these events. God is a God
of mercy and of love in the Old Testament as well as He is in the New
Testament.

CHAPTER 8

THEME: God's past dealings give assurance for the future

In this section of the restating of the Law, we come now to the portion dealing with religious and national regulations, which will be continued through chapter 21.

> **All the commandments which I command thee this day shall ye observe to do, that ye may live, and multiply, and go in and possess the land which the LORD sware unto your fathers [Deut. 8:1].**

Here is the new generation, standing on the east bank of the Jordan River. They are ready to cross over into the land with high anticipation and hope. As Moses is preparing them to enter the land, he encourages them to obey God.

> **And thou shalt remember all the way which the LORD thy God led thee these forty years in the wilderness, to humble thee, and to prove thee, to know what was in thine heart, whether thou wouldest keep his commandments, or no [Deut. 8:2].**

God wants them to remember the past. They should see in the past that God has been dealing with them, that He has been testing and training them.

God wants us to remember our past, too. Paul put it like this for the believer: "Being confident of this very thing, that he which hath begun a good work in you will perform it until the day of Jesus Christ" (Phil. 1:6). We are to remember that God has led us and blessed us. Isn't this true for you? Can't you say that God has brought you up to this very moment? If He has done that in the past, He will continue to do so in the future. Remembering is for our encouragement. It is to give us assurance for the future.

Why did God test Israel in the wilderness? It was to humble them and to prove what was really in their hearts. That explains why God puts you and me through the mill. Sometimes He puts us in the furnace and heaps it on very hot. Why? To test us and to humble us. Little man is proud, he's cocky, he is self-confident, and, to be frank, he is an abomination! Listen to the boasting and bragging and the pride with which little man walks the earth. So God must take His own people and put them through the mill in order to humble them and to prove them.

You know, testing really proves the metal. Tests will reveal whether or not a person is really a child of God. Our churches today are filled with affluent people who have never been tested. I can't tell whether or not they are genuine. The man who has been tested is the man in whom you can have confidence.

> **And he humbled thee, and suffered thee to hunger, and fed thee with manna, which thou knewest not, neither did thy fathers know; that he might make thee know that man doth not live by bread only, but by every word that proceedeth out of the mouth of the LORD doth man live [Deut. 8:3].**

Our Lord quoted this verse when He was tempted in the wilderness (Matt. 4:4 and Luke 4:4). If the Lord Jesus had not quoted this, we would probably pass by the great spiritual lesson that is here. God has been good to us. He has blessed us in many, many ways with material things. The important lesson is that God gives us those things in order that we might see that there is a spiritual wealth, the Word of God. It is the Word of God that is the real wealth for the child of God today.

> **Thy raiment waxed not old upon thee, neither did thy foot swell, these forty years [Deut. 8:4].**

Here is a strange, marvelous, miraculous statement! Imagine having a suit of clothes that would not wear out. I know the ladies would not like this at all. Year after year the wife could tell her hubby that she needed a new dress, and year after year the husband could say that the one she was wearing looked brand new. I tell you, after that went on for forty years, the women would be pretty far behind in the styles. However, in the wilderness the styles didn't change; so it really didn't make any difference. Seriously, this is marvelous; it is a miracle.

"Neither did thy foot swell, these forty years." A missionary doctor explained to me that out in the Orient where he served, the people had a sameness of diet. They did not get all the vitamins they needed; so they would show the manifestations of beriberi. One of the symptoms is a swelling of the feet. Now, you see, Israel got all their vitamins. They got all the nourishment that they needed. What did these folk eat for forty years? Why, it was manna. God fed them with manna, which was a miracle food. It provided everything they needed for the nourishment of their bodies.

Spiritual manna is the Word of God. It is a wonderful food. It will supply all your needs. I marvel at the letters I receive that attest to this. Someone will say that when I spoke on a certain chapter, that passage brought comfort to his heart. Someone else will write that he was in sin and had gotten away from God, had become cold and indifferent, and that passage from the Word of God brought him back. Someone else writes to say he listened and was saved. You see, friend, you won't get any swelling of the feet if you will read the Word of God. In other words, the Bible will meet your individual needs, whatever they may be. This is manna.

God promised temporal blessings to the nation Israel if they would serve Him.

Thou shalt also consider in thine heart, that, as a man chasteneth his son, so the LORD thy God chasteneth thee.

Therefore thou shalt keep the commandments of the LORD thy God, to walk in his ways, and to fear him.

For the LORD thy God bringeth thee into a good land, a land of brooks of water, of fountains and depths that spring out of valleys and hills;

A land of wheat, and barley, and vines, and fig trees, and pomegranates; a land of oil olive, and honey;

A land wherein thou shalt eat bread without scarceness, thou shalt not lack any thing in it; a land whose stones are iron, and out of whose hills thou mayest dig brass [Deut. 8:5-9].

God does not give this promise to Christians today. I would have you note this. There is a lopsided notion that if you are a faithful Christian, God will prosper you in temporal things. My friend, that is not true. God promised to prosper Israel in the land. He does not promise to prosper the Christian in the things of this world.

Now I know that there are Christians who are outstanding, successful businessmen. They say they took God into partnership, and God blessed them abundantly. He does do that, and we praise Him for it. But that is not what He has promised to do. This is the promise to the Christian: "Blessed be the God and Father of our Lord Jesus Christ, who hath blessed us with all spiritual blessings in heavenly places in Christ" (Eph. 1:3). He has promised us spiritual blessings. There is no verse in the New Testament which promises temporal blessing to the child of God today.

May I also add that although God does not promise temporal blessings, He sometimes does add them. God does this for some, but not for all. There are wonderful Christians whom the Lord has blessed financially. Some of them have been a great help to us in broadcasting the Word of God by radio. But I also want to say that some of the choicest children of God today have been blessed with spiritual blessings and not with the things of this world. They seem to be the happiest, and they seem actually to do more for God than anyone else. Certainly they have been a blessing to this poor preacher and a blessing to the cause of Christ in the world.

One of the major distinctions between the nation Israel in the Old Testament and the church in the New Testament is that God promised Israel temporal blessings and He promises us spiritual blessings. If you keep this straight it will prevent a great deal of heartache. Also, it will cause a great many children of God to rejoice rather than to lapse into a backslidden condition. My friend, if you are on a low economic level, cash in on some of your spiritual blessings so that you may enjoy the riches He has promised you.

> **When thou hast eaten and art full, then thou shalt bless the LORD thy God for the good land which he hath given thee.**
>
> **Beware that thou forget not the LORD thy God, in not keeping his commandments, and his judgments, and his statutes, which I command thee this day [Deut. 8:10–11].**

He continues his warning to Israel for the coming days of prosperity.

> **Then thine heart be lifted up, and thou forget the LORD thy God, which brought thee forth out of the land of Egypt, from the house of bondage;**
>
> **Who led thee through that great and terrible wilderness, wherein were fiery serpents, and scorpions, and drought, where there was no water; who brought thee forth water out of the rock of flint;**
>
> **Who fed thee in the wilderness with manna, which thy fathers knew not, that he might humble thee, and that he might prove thee, to do thee good at thy latter end [Deut. 8:14–16].**

At the "latter end," in the future Millennium, God promises to make Israel the leading nation with earthly blessings. God has not promised that to the church, my friend; so don't appropriate that promise for yourself. The Lord Jesus said, ". . . I go to prepare a place for you. And if I go and prepare a place for you, I will come again, and receive you unto myself; that where I am, there ye may be also" (John 14:2–3). The hope of the child of God today is that Christ is coming to take us out of this world. The hope of Israel is in this world. That distinction is of utmost importance.

If you try to mix these promises, it will cause utter confusion. Too many so-called theologians use a blender. They put the whole Bible into a blender, and they really mix it up! If you let the Bible stand as it is, you will see that God is very specific when He makes promises.

> **And thou say in thine heart, My power and the might of mine hand hath gotten me this wealth.**
>
> **But thou shalt remember the LORD thy God: for it is he that giveth thee power to get wealth, that he may establish his covenant which he sware unto thy fathers, as it is this day [Deut. 8:17–18].**

When the nation of Israel is in the land and is being prospered, then you can know it is obeying God. When it is not prospering in that land, it is an indication that it is not obeying God. Look at Israel today and make your own decision.

> **And it shall be, if thou do at all forget the LORD thy God, and walk after other gods, and serve them, and worship them, I testify against you this day that ye shall surely perish.**
>
> **As the nations which the LORD destroyeth before your face, so shall ye perish; because ye would not be obedient unto the voice of the LORD your God [Deut. 8:19–20].**

CHAPTER 9

God is reviewing for this new generation the past of the nation Israel. Their past was not good. God did not save them because they were good. He didn't call them because they were an outstanding nation. They were not.

God has not saved us because we are outstanding, or superior, or even good. The only kind of people God is saving is bad people. I am reminded of an incident when I was walking behind some members of the church I was serving. As we were walking through a park, a bum begged them for some money. We had encouraged our members to send such people to the mission where they would be helped. But this fellow didn't want that—he wanted money to buy wine. When I came along, the beggar told me that the folk ahead, who had gone into the church, thought they were better than anybody else. I answered him, "It's quite interesting that you say they think they are better than anyone else. I happen to know them, and I remember the day they came to Christ. Do you know why they came?" He looked at me in amazement. "They came because they thought they were *worse* than anybody else. They thought they were sinners and needed a Savior. That is why they came to Christ." You see, he had the idea, which is commonly expressed, that the church is made up of people who think they are better than other folk. Now that may be true in some cases. If it is true, the church is certainly not a church in the New Testament sense. God saves us because we are bad, because we are sinners.

Hear, O Israel: Thou art to pass over Jordan this day, to go in to possess nations greater and mightier than thyself, cities great and fenced up to heaven [Deut. 9:1].

"This day" does not refer to a twenty-four hour day, but to the time when they will enter the land.

A people great and tall, the children of the Anakims, whom thou knowest, and of whom thou hast heard say, Who can stand before the children of Anak! [Deut. 9:2].

God gives a report on the land which is worse than the report the spies had brought back. God knew the land and God knew who was in the land, yet God had told them to go in. They had refused to go in because they didn't believe God. God knew that the people there were giants. He knew all the difficulties. He had promised to go into the land with them.

It was Martin Luther who said, "One with God is a majority." My friend, if you are with God, you are with the majority. Actually, Christians belong to a minority group down here in this world. But I'll tell you something the world doesn't know: with God, we are a majority. One with God is a majority.

Understand therefore this day, that the LORD thy God is he which goeth over before thee; as a consuming fire he shall destroy them, and he shall bring them down before thy face: so shalt thou drive them out, and destroy them quickly, as the LORD hath said unto thee [Deut. 9:3].

God takes the responsibility of putting them out of the land. God is the Landlord. He is the Creator. He has a right to do this. When I hear a fellow who is liberal in his theology complain about this, I feel like saying, "You little pip-squeak, you keep quiet. You and I are just little creatures down here." God is the sovereign Creator; we are the creatures.

Speak not thou in thine heart, after that the LORD thy God hath cast them out from before thee, saying, For my righteousness the LORD hath brought me in to possess this land: but for the wickedness of these nations the LORD doth drive them out from before thee [Deut. 9:4].

God is saying that He is driving the other nations out because they are wicked nations—not because the people He is putting in there are righteous. God makes that abundantly clear.

> Not for thy righteousness, or for the uprightness of thine heart, dost thou go to possess their land: but for the wickedness of these nations the LORD thy God doth drive them out from before thee, and that he may perform the word which the LORD sware unto thy fathers, Abraham, Isaac, and Jacob [Deut. 9:5].

God did not come down to deliver Israel because they were a wonderful people. He knew all the time that they were a stiff-necked people, but He heard their cry in Egypt. And friend, if you recognize that you are a sinner and need a Savior, then you will need to cry to Him for salvation. He will hear you. Do you know why? Not because of who you are, but for Christ's sake. If you will turn to Christ in faith, He will save you.

> Understand therefore, that the LORD thy God giveth thee not this good land to possess it for thy righteousness; for thou art a stiffnecked people [Deut. 9:6].

Do you know that God does not save you and me because we are good? We are sinners. He saves us for Christ's sake, not for our sake. Friend, if you think that somehow or other God will find something in you that merits salvation, forget it, because you will be disappointed. God knows you, and He says He can't find anything righteous in you at all. It is for Christ's sake that God saves us, and God finds everything we need in Him. How wonderful that is! You see that in this passage of Deuteronomy there is the seed for the gospel of the grace of God.

ISRAEL'S PAST FAILURE

> Remember, and forget not, how thou provokedst the LORD thy God to wrath in the wilderness: from the day that thou didst depart out of the land of Egypt, until ye

came unto this place, ye have been rebellious against the LORD [Deut. 9:7].

Moses directs them back over their past history and refers specifically to the time when they made the golden calf. If we turn back to Exodus 32:4 we read, "And he received them at their hand . . . ," referring to the golden earrings. The women, and the men, too, took off their golden earrings and gave them to Aaron. Those golden earrings were a sign of idolatry (generally they were worn in one ear only). These people had lapsed back into idolatry very quickly. Aaron took the golden earrings, and with a graving tool he fashioned a molten calf. And they said, "These be thy gods, O Israel, which brought thee up out of the land of Egypt." Now God calls them to remember this. God reminded them of that again in Psalm 106:19. "They made a calf in Horeb, and worshiped the molten image." God asked them to remember, but they forgot.

Also in Horeb ye provoked the LORD to wrath, so that the LORD was angry with you to have destroyed you [Deut. 9:8].

Moses goes on with his narrative:

And the LORD said unto me, Arise, get thee down quickly from hence; for thy people which thou hast brought forth out of Egypt have corrupted themselves; they are quickly turned aside out of the way which I commanded them; they have made them a molten image [Deut. 9:12].

At the very time they were making the molten calf, Moses was on the Mount getting the Commandments, and two of these commandments were against that very thing: "Thou shalt have no other gods. Thou shalt not make unto thee any graven image." Notice that God says to Moses, "They're your people. You brought them out of Egypt." Moses will answer that in just a moment.

Furthermore the LORD spake unto me, saying, I have seen this people, and, behold, it is a stiffnecked people [Deut. 9:13].

The Lord repeats this—He knew all the time that Israel was a stiffnecked people. He knows you and me also, and can probably say the same thing about us.

Let me alone, that I may destroy them, and blot out their name from under heaven: and I will make of thee a nation mightier and greater than they [Deut. 9:14].

This must have been a temptation for Moses, but he resisted it. His pleading for Israel is recorded in Exodus 33:12–17. Moses would not go up into the land without the presence of the Lord. He said, "If thy presence go not with me, carry us not up hence." Moses identified himself with the people.

When Moses came down from the Mount, he saw what they had done.

And I looked, and, behold, ye had sinned against the LORD your God, and had made you a molten calf: ye had turned aside quickly out of the way which the LORD had commanded you [Deut. 9:16].

At the very moment when God was giving them the Commandments, they were turning from Him—yet they were saying they would obey Him. People can be more phony in religion than in anything else. It seems to be something that is characteristic of the human nature. Even people who are really sincere are as phony as can be. We all need to pray the prayer of the psalmist, "Search me, O God, and know my heart: try me, and know my thoughts: and see if there be any wicked way in me, and lead me in the way everlasting" (Ps. 139:23–24). Every child of God needs to pray this. Paul has this admonition for the believers: "Examine yourselves, whether ye be in the faith; prove your own selves. Know ye not your own selves, how that Jesus Christ is in you, except ye be reprobates?" (2 Cor. 13:5). Check whether you are in the faith or not. I believe and I preach the security of the believer, my friend. I believe that the believer is secure. But I also believe and preach the insecurity of the make-believer. There are a lot of make-believers. We need to search our hearts, every one of us.

> **And I took the two tables, and cast them out of my two hands, and brake them before your eyes.**

> **And I fell down before the LORD, as at the first, forty days and forty nights: I did neither eat bread, nor drink water, because of all your sins which ye sinned, in doing wickedly in the sight of the LORD, to provoke him to anger [Deut. 9:17–18].**

I want you to notice that Moses knew God. The psalmist says, "He made known his ways unto Moses, his acts unto the children of Israel" (Ps. 103:7). The children of Israel saw the mountain smoke, they saw the judgment of God, they saw His glory, but they did not know Him. Moses knew Him! Moses knew His ways.

Moses understood two things about God which are revealed here. They are paradoxical, but they are not contradictory.

Moses knew that God hates sin. May I say to you that we today do not have the faintest conception of how God hates sin and how He intends to punish it. Moses went down on his face before God and fasted and cried out to God for forty days and forty nights! Why? Because Moses knew the ways of God. He knew how God hates sin.

The average Christian today does not seem to realize how God hates sin in his life. My friend, God never ignores a sin we commit. God will deal with sin in your life and in my life. I have been a pastor for a long time, and I have observed church people over the years. I want to say to you that I have watched people in the church play fast and loose with God. I have seen them cut corners and put up a front. The days melt into years, and then I have seen the hand of God move in judgment on their lives. Sometimes the judgment has been extremely severe. I can especially remember a man who came to me and actually dropped down on his knees and cried out that he just could not stand what God was putting him through. He had lost his children, lost his family. I can remember him as a young upstart, a young married man, who thought he could play fast and loose with God. God hates sin. God punishes sin.

Moses also knew the mercy of God. Moses comes to God because he trusts in His mercy. God will punish sin, but, my friend, we do not comprehend how wonderful He is. He is so gracious. He extends mercy to the sinner. He has extended His mercy to you, I am sure. I know He has to me. And the Lord extended mercy to Israel. Listen:

> **For I was afraid of the anger and hot displeasure, wherewith the LORD was wroth against you to destroy you. But the LORD hearkened unto me at that time also [Deut. 9:19].**

God did not hear the prayer of Moses because of who he was. God heard his prayer because He is merciful. Paul makes this clear in Romans 9:15, "For he saith to Moses, I will have mercy on whom I will have mercy, and I will have compassion on whom I will have compassion." God is sovereign, and He sovereignly extends His mercy. How wonderful He is. You and I do not fully comprehend those two attributes of God: His hatred of sin and His mercy.

> **And the LORD was very angry with Aaron to have destroyed him: and I prayed for Aaron also the same time.**

> **And I took your sin, the calf which ye had made, and burnt it with fire, and stamped it, and ground it very small, even until it was as small as dust: and I cast the dust thereof into the brook that descended out of the mount [Deut. 9:20–21].**

If this incident weren't so tragic, it would be humorous. Moses makes the people drink their idol.

And at Taberah, and at Massah, and at Kibroth-hattaavah, ye provoked the Lord to wrath.

Likewise, when the Lord sent you from Kadesh-barnea, saying, Go up and possess the land which I have given you; then ye rebelled against the commandment of the Lord your God, and ye believed him not, nor hearkened to his voice.

Ye have been rebellious against the Lord from the day that I knew you [Deut. 9:22–24].

This is a summary. There never was a day when these people were really found faithful to God. What a picture! We tend to point to them in criticism, but what about the believer today? I am afraid there are many of us, even in conservative churches, who are not faithful to God for a single day. We boast that we are sound in the faith—sound all right—sound asleep!

Thus I fell down before the Lord forty days and forty nights, as I fell down at the first; because the Lord had said he would destroy you [Deut. 9:25].

This was after they refused to go into the land at Kadesh-barnea. Moses knew God. Moses knew that God judges sin.

I prayed therefore unto the Lord, and said, O Lord God, destroy not thy people and thine inheritance, which thou hast redeemed through thy greatness, which thou hast brought forth out of Egypt with a mighty hand.

Remember thy servants, Abraham, Isaac, and Jacob; look not unto the stubbornness of this people, nor to their wickedness, nor to their sin:

Lest the land whence thou broughtest us out say, Because the Lord was not able to bring them into the land which he promised them, and because he hated them, he hath brought them out to slay them in the wilderness.

Yet they are thy people and thine inheritance, which thou broughtest out by thy mighty power and by thy stretched out arm [Deut. 9:26-29].

Moses knew how to pray. I wish I knew how to pray like that! Remember that back in verse 12 God said, "For thy people which thou hast brought forth out of Egypt have corrupted themselves." Now imagine Moses saying to God that He has made a mistake! Moses says, "They are not my people; they are Yours. I didn't bring them out of Egypt; You did. They belong to You." Moses reminds God that the people in the land would think He was unable to bring Israel into the land—that He was able to bring Israel out of Egypt, but He was not able to bring them into the land. That kind of praying moves the hand of God. Here Israel stands, ready now to enter the land which reveals that Moses knew how to pray!

CHAPTER 10

THEME: God sent Israel to Egypt; God brought them out of Egypt

As Moses has said in his prayer, Israel belongs to God; they are His inheritance. He will not destroy them because of their sin but graciously give them again the Ten Commandments, written by Himself.

> At that time the LORD said unto me, Hew thee two tables of stone like unto the first, and come up unto me into the mount, and make thee an ark of wood.
>
> And I will write on the tables the words that were in the first tables which thou brakest, and thou shalt put them in the ark [Deut. 10:1–2].

Moses brought the tables of stone down and placed them in the ark. Then the children of Israel continued on their journey.

> At that time the LORD separated the tribe of Levi, to bear the ark of the covenant of the LORD, to stand before the LORD to minister unto him, and to bless in his name, unto this day.
>
> Wherefore Levi hath no part nor inheritance with his brethren; the LORD is his inheritance, according as the LORD thy God promised him [Deut. 10:8–9].

There are great spiritual lessons in this for us. As Levi was the priestly tribe, so today the church is a kingdom of priests. That is, every believer in Jesus Christ is a priest. I am not a Roman Catholic priest, but I am a "catholic" priest (as is every believer in Christ) in the sense that *catholic* means "general." The New Testament priest is to offer himself to God for worship, intercession, and service (Rom. 12:1–2). And he is to exercise a gift as a priest according to 1 Corinthians 12. And every believer, as a priest, has a gift to exercise in the church.

Notice that the tribe of Levi was to have no material inheritance. God was their inheritance. God had promised to give land, a certain amount of acreage, to the other tribes. And when He blessed them, it was temporal blessing. He did not promise that to Levi. This is also the position of the believer today. Like Levi, our inheritance is in God. We are blessed with all spiritual blessings in the heavenlies.

And now, Israel, what doth the LORD thy God require of thee, but to fear the LORD thy God, to walk in all his ways, and to love him, and to serve the LORD thy God with all thy heart and with all thy soul [Deut. 10:12].

Now do not make the mistake of thinking this is the gospel. It is not the gospel. You and I ought to thank God for that, because if it depended on this, you and I wouldn't be blessed very much.

To keep the commandments of the LORD, and his statutes, which I command thee this day for thy good? [Deut. 10:13].

If Israel had kept them, they would have been blessed. When they broke them, judgment came upon them. God, for fifteen hundred years, demonstrated through Israel to the world and to you and me that He cannot save people by Law. These people under favorable circumstances, in a land geared to the Law, were unable to keep it. And if they were unable to keep it, then you and I are unable to keep it. Thank God, He saves by grace today. In fact, grace has always been His method. In the Old Testament He never saved anyone by Law. They were saved by His mercy and grace to them, looking forward to the coming of Christ to die on the Cross to take away their sins.

He doth execute the judgment of the fatherless and widow, and loveth the stranger, in giving him food and raiment [Deut. 10:18].

God loved the stranger. And He reminded these people that they had been strangers in the land of Egypt.

Love ye therefore the stranger: for ye were strangers in the land of Egypt.

Thou shalt fear the LORD thy God; him shalt thou serve, and to him shalt thou cleave, and swear by his name [Deut. 10:19–20].

The Lord Jesus quoted this to answer Satan, you remember. Our Lord certainly was familiar with the Book of Deuteronomy, as probably every Israelite was in that day.

Thy fathers went down into Egypt with threescore and ten persons; and now the LORD thy God hath made thee as the stars of heaven for multitude [Deut. 10:22].

The evident blessing of God was upon them. He sent them down into Egypt; He brought them out of Egypt. God was responsible, and He didn't mind taking that responsibility.

CHAPTER 11

THEME: The Promised Land unlike Egypt; principle of occupancy of the land

God talks to them here about the land they are about to enter. The Promised Land will not be at all like Egypt. And God will give them the principles required for occupancy of the land.

A CALL TO COMMITMENT

Therefore thou shalt love the LORD thy God, and keep his charge, and his statutes, and his judgments, and his commandments, always [Deut. 11:1].

The response to the love of God is obedience.

Therefore shall ye keep all the commandments which I command you this day, that ye may be strong, and go in and possess the land, whither ye go to possess it;

And that ye may prolong your days in the land, which the LORD sware unto your fathers to give unto them and to their seed, a land that floweth with milk and honey [Deut. 11:8–9].

They were accustomed to irrigated fields down in Egypt.

For the land, whither thou goest in to possess it, is not as the land of Egypt, from whence ye came out, where thou sowedst thy seed, and wateredst it with thy foot, as a garden of herbs [Deut. 11:10].

When I was in Egypt I was told that the rainfall there is less than one inch a year. Now that is not much rainfall! I've been to a place in the

Hawaiian Islands where the rainfall is over 100 inches a year. That is quite a difference. Obviously, Egypt was dependent upon irrigation.

PRINCIPLE OF OCCUPANCY OF THE LAND

But the land, whither ye go to possess it, is a land of hills and valleys, and drinketh water of the rain of heaven:

A land which the LORD thy God careth for: the eyes of the LORD thy God are always upon it, from the beginning of the year even unto the end of the year.

And it shall come to pass, if ye shall hearken diligently unto my commandments which I command you this day, to love the LORD your God, and to serve him with all your heart and with all your soul.

That I will give you the rain of your land in his due season, the first rain and the latter rain, that thou mayest gather in thy corn, and thy wine, and thine oil.

And I will send grass in thy fields for thy cattle, that thou mayest eat and be full [Deut. 11:11–15].

The land these people were going to enter would be a little difficult to irrigate because it was hilly. Of course they didn't have the equipment for it in that day. The land would depend upon the rain from heaven. God did this purposely. He put them on a land that had to depend upon Him for rainfall. This would draw the people closer to God.

The reason that land is desolate today, as we shall see in Deuteronomy, is because the judgment of God is upon it. The minute water is put into that soil, the desert blossoms as a rose. It is water that it needs, and they are having trouble with water there even today. God told them that they would be dependent upon rain. If they would obey Him, He would bless them with the former and latter rains; that is, the fall and spring rainfall. By looking at that land you can see the spiritual condition of the people.

In an affluent society such as we live in today, where things come so easily, I am afraid that people assume God has nothing in the world to do with it. I do not understand why people think that if things come easily, they have done it; if things come with difficulty, then God must be in it. Well, God is the One who provides for all our physical needs. Whether things come to us easily or with difficulty, He still is the Provider.

For if ye shall diligently keep all these commandments which I command you, to do them, to love the LORD your God, to walk in all his ways, and to cleave unto him [Deut. 11:22].

The great principle of their occupancy of the land is given here.

Then will the LORD drive out all these nations from before you, and ye shall possess greater nations and mightier than yourselves.

Every place whereon the soles of your feet shall tread shall be yours: from the wilderness and Lebanon, from the river, the river Euphrates, even unto the uttermost sea shall your coast be.

There shall no man be able to stand before you: for the LORD your God shall lay the fear of you and the dread of you upon all the land that ye shall tread upon, as he hath said unto you [Deut. 11:23–25].

You will notice that the land is a gift from God. He has given to them a land which is much greater than anything they have ever occupied. It was from the river Euphrates to the Mediterranean Sea, and from Lebanon all the way south into the desert that they had come through. This was approximately 300,000 square miles. They have never occupied more than about 30,000 square miles of it, even at the time when the kingdom reached its zenith under David and Solomon.

"Every place whereon the soles of your feet shall tread shall be yours." It had been given to them by God and it was theirs, but they failed to walk upon it, claim it, and enjoy it. God told Joshua the same thing. He told him that the land was right there before them and that it belonged to Israel. But He told them they had to go in and walk up and down in the land. They had to possess it.

Why is there such a difference in believers today? Some Christians are sitting on the side lines and are poverty stricken spiritually. Others are fabulously rich spiritually. God makes it clear that He has blessed all believers with spiritual blessings in the heavenlies in Christ Jesus. Some believers claim those blessings; some do not. Some believers enjoy those blessings; some do not. It is a matter of appropriating that which we already possess.

Behold, I set before you this day a blessing and a curse [Deut. 11:26].

Israel was commanded to obey. Obedience was the very nub of the matter.

A blessing, if ye obey the commandments of the LORD your God, which I command you this day [Deut. 11:27].

Obedience is something which has been dropped into the background today. I believe in the grace of God. I preach the grace of God. We are saved by grace, we are kept by grace, we grow by the grace of God. We are going to get to heaven by the grace of God. When we've been there ten thousand years, it will still be by the grace of God. But, my friend, there are great spiritual blessings today which you are going to miss if you are not obedient to Him. Jesus told us, "If ye love me, keep my commandments" (John 14:15). Obedience offers a personal, wonderful, glorious relationship with God.

The opposite is also true. Disobedience brings with it a curse.

And a curse, if ye will not obey the commandments of the LORD your God, but turn aside out of the way which I

**command you this day, to go after other gods, which ye
have not known [Deut. 11:28].**

You will notice that the great issue over which God is pleading with
Israel is idolatry. There was always the danger that they would turn
from Jehovah, their God, and lapse back into idolatry.

CHAPTER 12

THEME: Israel permitted only one place to worship

L ater in the history of Israel, God chose Jerusalem as the place where the temple was to be built. They were to go there to worship God. Why didn't God permit the worship in every other place? I think the reason is obvious. There was idolatry in the land, and they were commanded to destroy it. Because they did not destroy it, they were commanded to assemble in one place for worship. This unified their worship and brought them closer together as a nation. They were one when they went up to Jerusalem for the feasts.

Today we do not need to meet in one place to worship God. The Lord Jesus told the Samaritan woman the reason why this is true. "Jesus saith unto her, Woman, believe me, the hour cometh, when ye shall neither in this mountain, nor yet at Jerusalem, worship the Father. Ye worship ye know not what: we know what we worship: for salvation is of the Jews. But the hour cometh, and now is, when the true worshippers shall worship the Father in spirit and in truth; for the Father seeketh such to worship him. God is a Spirit: and they that worship him must worship him in spirit and in truth" (John 4:21–24).

Believers do not meet in one *place* to worship God today; we meet around One *Person* and that Person is the Lord Jesus Christ. That is the important thing to keep in mind today. The name of your church doesn't make the difference. The denomination or lack of denomination of your church doesn't make the difference. The all-important question is this: do you meet around the person of Jesus Christ? Now, friends, if you don't, that is idolatry, because then you are meeting around something that is replacing Christ. If you are meeting to socialize or be entertained, that is idolatry. The thing that is to draw us together into a oneness is the person of Jesus Christ. How important that is!

These are the statutes and judgments, which ye shall observe to do in the land, which the LORD God of thy

fathers giveth thee to possess it, all the days that ye live upon the earth.

Ye shall utterly destroy all the places, wherein the nations which ye shall possess served their gods, upon the high mountains, and upon the hills, and under every green tree:

And ye shall overthrow their altars, and break their pillars, and burn their groves with fire; and ye shall hew down the graven images of their gods, and destroy the names of them out of that place.

Ye shall not do so unto the LORD your God [Deut. 12:1–4].

The reason the judgments of God came upon Israel, one after the other in the times of the judges, was because the people had lapsed into idolatry. Then that great prophet Elijah leveled his message against idolatry in the land. The reason Israel went into the Babylonian captivity was idolatry. The warning in the last book of the Old Testament is about the danger of idolatry.

We should not think we are immune to idolatry today. We tend to think we are such enlightened folk that we would not fall down and worship an idol. Can we be so sure about that, friends? Anything, *anything* that comes between our souls and God becomes an idol. I know a young man whom I saw grow up in the church and seemingly become a sweet Christian. Later he became a member of a large corporation. Because he had wonderful ability, he began to move up in the organization. The farther he moved up in the corporation, the farther he moved away from God. Today his job comes first. I was holding meetings in a distant city where he lives, and he invited Mrs. McGee and me for dinner, for old time's sake. He made it very clear to me that he would not be able to come to any of the meetings because of his business. Business, his position, his advancements—they had become his idol, his god. Talk about worship! He fell down before that idol seven days a week!

Anything that comes between your soul and your God is your idol.

But unto the place which the LORD your God shall choose out of all your tribes to put his name there, even unto his habitation shall ye seek, and thither thou shalt come [Deut. 12:5].

Eventually, the designated place was Jerusalem. But even before that, Israel was to worship in one place only. There was to be one place for their burnt offerings, sacrifices, tithes, and vows. The tithes of food which they brought before the Lord had to be eaten in this one place.

Notwithstanding thou mayest kill and eat flesh in all thy gates, whatsoever thy soul lusteth after, according to the blessing of the LORD thy God which he hath given thee: the unclean and the clean may eat thereof, as of the roebuck, and as of the hart.

Only ye shall not eat the blood; ye shall pour it upon the earth as water [Deut. 12:15–16].

There was also food which they ate at home. This was not a part of their worship, but this, too, was regulated by dietary laws. In Chapter 14 we will find an extensive list of clean and unclean animals. A person did not need to be ceremonially clean to be able to eat at home. Also, in addition to the animals which were sacrificial animals, he could eat wild game so long as it was a clean animal. The stipulation given was that the blood was not to be eaten. In contrast, anything that was an offering to the Lord had to be eaten before the Lord in the one place which God would designate.

If the place which the LORD thy God hath chosen to put his name there be too far from thee, then thou shalt kill of thy herd and of thy flock, which the LORD hath given thee, as I have commanded thee, and thou shalt eat in thy gates whatsoever thy soul lustest after.

Even as the roebuck and the hart is eaten, so thou shalt eat them: the unclean and the clean shall eat of them alike.

Only be sure that thou eat not the blood: for the blood is the life; and thou mayest not eat the life with the flesh.

Thou shalt not eat it; thou shalt pour it upon the earth as water.

Thou shalt not eat it; that it may go well with thee, and with thy children after thee, when thou shalt do that which is right in the sight of the LORD [Deut. 12:21–25].

In Leviticus 17, while Israel was in the wilderness camp, they were told that every time an ox, or lamb, or goat was killed, it had to be brought to the door of the tabernacle and the priest would sprinkle the blood upon the altar and would offer the fat as a sweet savor to God. This was to prevent them from making any offering to devils. After they settle in the land, it is obvious that many people will live too far away from Jerusalem to bring every animal there before they kill it for food. So the Lord tells them again that an animal may be killed for food, but they shall not eat the blood of the animal. The blood represents the life, which is the reason that Scripture puts such an emphasis on the blood of Jesus Christ.

When the LORD thy God shall cut off the nations from before thee, whither thou goest to possess them, and thou succeedest them, and dwellest in their land;

Take heed to thyself that thou be not snared by following them, after that they be destroyed from before thee; and that thou inquire not after their gods, saying, How did these nations serve their gods? even so will I do likewise.

Thou shalt not do so unto the LORD thy God: for every abomination to the LORD, which he hateth, have they

done unto their gods; for even their sons and their daughters they have burnt in the fire to their gods [Deut. 12:29-31].

They are told over and over again that they are to destroy the nations which are in the land so that they do not become ensnared by them. These nations were idolatrous. In the worship of Baal, as in the worship of many pagan religions, they had that most cruel practice of offering their own children. They would heat an idol red-hot and then drop their babies into the arms of this red-hot idol. I can't think of anything more horrible than that. God says He hates such a practice. It is an abomination to Him. I find that God hates many things that I hate. I hope that I can learn more and more to hate what He hates and love what He loves.

What thing soever I command you, observe to do it: thou shalt not add thereto, nor diminish from it [Deut. 12:32].

They are to give heed to these commandments which the Lord gives them. If they disobey God, God will treat them as He treats the other nations. God doesn't watch the actions of some people and disregard others. I have never understood why some Christians think they can get by with certain things that other people do not get by with. Sin is sin. If Israel does not obey the Lord, she will not be spared. So the encouragement for them is to observe to do what the Lord commands them.

CHAPTER 13

This is a very important chapter because it deals with false prophets and false gods. When we get to chapter 18 of Deuteronomy, we will find the test which would identify a false prophet. Israel had no problem in detecting the false prophets because they had a biblical, God-given test that surely would ferret them out. However, the chapter before us deals with the action that was to be taken against anyone who attempted to lead God's people away from Him by introducing false religions.

> If there arise among you a prophet, or a dreamer of dreams, and giveth thee a sign or a wonder,
>
> And the sign or the wonder come to pass, whereof he spake unto thee, saying, Let us go after other gods, which thou hast not known, and let us serve them;
>
> Thou shalt not hearken unto the words of that prophet, or that dreamer of dreams: for the LORD your God proveth you, to know whether ye love the LORD your God with all your heart and with all your soul.
>
> Ye shall walk after the LORD your God, and fear him, and keep his commandments, and obey his voice, and ye shall serve him, and cleave unto him [Deut. 13:1–4].

This is pertinent for today. People ask me how I explain the fact that some of the false prophets today are accurate part of the time. Or they ask me to explain how some people seem to be healed in certain meetings. Well, I don't explain it. To begin with, I think there would probably be a natural explanation in many instances, but even if there is something supernatural, God has warned that this can be accomplished through false prophets. It is well for us to mark that. God says that when a false prophet comes along and performs signs which come to pass, we are not to believe him if he denies the great truths of the Christian faith. That is the great principle which is put down here, and that is very important.

> **And that prophet, or that dreamer of dreams, shall be put to death; because he hath spoken to turn you away from the LORD your God, which brought you out of the land of Egypt, and redeemed you out of the house of bondage, to thrust thee out of the way which the LORD thy God commanded thee to walk in. So shalt thou put the evil away from the midst of thee [Deut. 13:5].**

Notice that any false prophet who attempted to take the people into some false cult or false religion was to be stoned to death. Does that sound extreme? Does that sound severe? Such a false prophet is like a cancer, and a cancer must be cut out as soon as possible—I know that from personal experience. God here is the Great Physician and He says the cancer must be cut out from among His people.

This reveals the mind of God concerning false prophets who lead the people to false gods and false religion. I can remember when I was a boy that the reading of the Bible in the schoolroom was a normal procedure. I don't think it was particularly meaningful to me at that time, yet I understood it was the Word of God and that impressed me. Today we have let the unbeliever come in, the cults, and those who oppose Christianity and the Bible, and they have taken over so that Bible reading and prayer are no longer permitted in public schools.

God laid down these rules to prevent this from happening in Israel. If one appeared in Israel who was attempting to take God's people away from the worship of God, that person was to be put to death.

Some soft-hearted and soft-headed folk will say this is too extreme. God understood how terrible it would be if false prophets were permitted to multiply and to lead Israel into idolatry. History reveals that Israel did not obey God and they did permit this to happen. If you want to know how bad it was for God's people in that day, read the story of Ahab and Jezebel who plunged God's people into idolatry.

This brought the judgment of God upon them so that eventually the northern kingdom was carried into captivity. That is how serious it is.

> **If thy brother, the son of thy mother, or thy son, or thy daughter, or the wife of thy bosom, or thy friend, which is as thine own soul, entice thee secretly, saying, Let us go and serve other gods, which thou hast not known, thou, nor thy fathers;**
>
> **Namely, of the gods of the people which are round about you, nigh unto thee, or far off from thee, from the one end of the earth even unto the other end of the earth;**
>
> **Thou shalt not consent unto him, nor hearken unto him; neither shall thine eye pity him, neither shalt thou spare, neither shalt thou conceal him:**
>
> **But thou shalt surely kill him; thine hand shall be first upon him to put him to death, and afterwards the hand of all the people [Deut. 13:6–9].**

This is extreme. This is radical. This sounds like a foreign language to the soft and affluent society in which we live. It is a serious matter for a man to be the first one to throw a stone in the execution that would stone his own brother to death. That seems very severe, but ultimately it would save many lives. When the northern kingdom went into idolatry, what happened? Literally thousands of them were slain, and most of the survivors were taken as slaves to the brutal nation of Assyria. Wouldn't it have been better if they had stoned the false prophets who led them into idolatry instead of a whole multitude being slain?

We see the same kind of thing in our nation today. We have so many soft-hearted and soft-headed judges who have no Christian background whatsoever. They do not think of our laws in the Christian context in which they were originally formulated—that is, obedience to law and a penalty exacted for disobedience. Our judges turn criminals loose to again prey on society. Right here in my town, a known criminal attacked seven women in one night. Several were killed, one was raped, others were hospitalized with severe injuries. Now wouldn't it be wiser for the criminal to be given the utmost penalty than for many innocent people to be murdered? God's way is the way that will save lives and protect a host of people. I am afraid that we have become so shortsighted that capital punishment sounds extreme to us today.

And thou shalt stone him with stones, that he die; because he hath sought to thrust thee away from the LORD thy God, which brought thee out of the land of Egypt, from the house of bondage [Deut. 13:10].

God exacts the death penalty. Today we feel that the death penalty is uncivilized. I guess the crowd who feels that way would call God uncivilized. I would like to ask that crowd where they got the little civilization and the little culture which they do have. All of it came from the Word of God, friends. Now we are moving away from the Word of God and folk think that is being more civilized. It is more dangerous to walk on the streets of the cities in the United States than it is to walk on the jungle trails of Africa. Why? Because we think the death penalty is uncivilized and so we have abolished it. Some time ago as I was walking by night on a jungle trail in the mountain regions of Venezuela, I felt safer than I do in Los Angeles, although they said there might be a few boa constrictors around. And I noticed that nobody locked their doors. I wondered whether they should send missionaries to us instead of our sending missionaries to them.

And all Israel shall hear, and fear, and shall do no more any such wickedness as this is among you [Deut. 13:11].

They were not to depart from the living and true God. As long as they would obey Him, there would be blessing. However, they failed to obey Him, and the judgments did come upon them—that is their story.

> If thou shalt hear say in one of thy cities, which the LORD thy God hath given thee to dwell there, saying,
>
> Certain men, the children of Belial, are gone out from among you, and have withdrawn the inhabitants of their city, saying, Let us go and serve other gods, which ye have not known;
>
> Then shalt thou inquire, and make search, and ask diligently; and, behold, if it be truth, and the thing certain, that such abomination is wrought among you [Deut. 13:12–14].

They were not to do anything rashly. A thorough investigation must be made and truth arrived at before any action was to be taken.

> Thou shalt surely smite the inhabitants of that city with the edge of the sword, destroying it utterly, and all that is therein, and the cattle thereof, with the edge of the sword.
>
> And thou shalt gather all the spoil of it into the midst of the street thereof, and shalt burn with fire the city, and all the spoil thereof every whit, for the LORD thy God: and it shall be an heap for ever; it shall not be built again [Deut. 13:15–16].

Again, this is severe. A city, an entire city, would be destroyed. Suppose there was someone in that city who hadn't gone into idolatry. Had they protested? Had they just sat by and done nothing? If they had done nothing about it, they were to be judged along with the rest.

There are too many Christians today who think that it is Christian to be silent. There are so many Christians who do not take a stand on important issues even when truth is at stake. You hear the old cliché, "Silence is golden." Friends, sometimes it is yellow—not golden—to remain silent and not to take a stand. The minority is to protest that which is wrong.

Everything in such a city was to be completely destroyed.

And there shall cleave nought of the cursed thing to thine hand: that the Lord may turn from the fierceness of his anger, and shew thee mercy, and have compassion upon thee, and multiply thee, as he hath sworn unto thy fathers [Deut. 13:17].

CHAPTER 14

THEME: Diet for Israel

Although Leviticus 11 and Deuteronomy 12 deal with the diet for God's people, we have in this chapter regulations that may be a little clearer than those in Leviticus. The reason for this is that the dietary law recorded in Leviticus has now been tested during the wilderness march for forty years.

PAGAN RITES FORBIDDEN

Ye are the children of the Lord your God: ye shall not cut yourselves, nor make any baldness between your eyes for the dead.

For thou art an holy people unto the Lord thy God, and the Lord hath chosen thee to be a peculiar people unto himself, above all the nations that are upon the earth [Deut. 14:1–2].

These were heathen, pagan practices in that day. We see the carry-over of this among certain tribes on the earth today who still disfigure their faces. It is a part of their worship, a part of their religion. God's people were never to do anything like that.

In my book, *Learning Through Leviticus,* I have gone into more detail regarding the clean and unclean animals. The diet which God gave to His people was more than just a religious ritual. There was actually a physical benefit from their observation of it. This has been tested down through the centuries.

When the plague broke out in Europe years ago, the Jewish population was hardly touched by the plague at all, while a large percentage of the gentile population died. So the people began to blame the Jews for the plague. Of course, they had nothing in the world to do with it, but their dietary habits and living habits had protected them from the plague.

We are living in a day of diets of all sorts. Everyone seems to be interested in diet. God has not given specific dietary laws for you and me. It makes no difference whether we eat meat or don't eat meat as far as our relationship to God is concerned. However if you observe these laws, you may stay in this world a little longer, and if you don't, it may get you into His presence a little sooner!

Now He will make it clear what animals are included and which are excluded:

> **Thou shalt not eat any abominable thing.**
>
> **These are the beasts which ye shall eat: the ox, the sheep, and the goat,**
>
> **The hart, and the roebuck, and the fallow deer, and the wild goat, and the pygarg, and the wild ox, and the chamois.**
>
> **And every beast that parteth the hoof, and cleaveth the cleft into two claws, and cheweth the cud among the beasts, that ye shall eat [Deut. 14:3–6].**

These were the clean animals which they could eat. There were two marks that identified the clean animals. These marks also teach us spiritual lessons.

The hoof of the animal was to be divided or separated. That could symbolize the walk of the believer. The separated hoof speaks of a separated life. Now I know that there is a lot of legalism which is brought into Christian conduct today. There are a great many people who don't restrict themselves to the Ten Commandments, but they have added about twenty-five others, and they live by them. I do not believe that is what God is indicating by the separated hoof. The word "cleave" actually has two opposite meanings. Cleaving can mean to break apart or break asunder, or it can mean to be attached to something. This is true also of separation. One can be separated *from* something or separated *unto* something. The important thing is not to be separated from certain activities or habits but to be separated unto *Christ*. When you are separated unto Christ and joined to Him, your "walk" will undergo a radical change.

The second mark of the clean animals was the chewing of the cud. The spiritual lesson here is that we should spend time in the Word of God. "But his delight is in the law of the LORD; and in his law doth he meditate day and night" (Ps. 1:2). The first verse starts out with "Blessed is the man." The blessed man delights in the Law of the Lord and meditates on it. That word "meditate" has the idea of chewing the cud. It is illustrated by the cow which has a complex stomach. As she grazes on the grass in the morning, it goes into one chamber of her stomach. In the heat of the day she lies down under a tree or stands in the shade, and chews her cud, which transfers that grass from one chamber to the other. Chewing the cud is rechewing the grass, going over it again. That is what we are to do with the Word of God—we are to go over and over it, meditating on it.

The unclean animals fail to meet these two requirements. Some chew the cud but do not have the divided hoof. The pig has the divided hoof but does not chew the cud. Such animals were designated as unclean and were not to be eaten.

Also certain marine life was designated as unclean:

These ye shall eat of all that are in the waters: all that have fins and scales shall ye eat:

And whatsoever hath not fins and scales ye may not eat; it is unclean unto you [Deut. 14:9–10].

Water creatures must be characterized by two visible marks—fins and scales—to be edible.

There follows a list of clean and unclean birds. There are a great number of people who try to put themselves back under the Mosaic Law, and they know a great deal about not eating pork. So when one of them begins to chide me about eating pork, I remind them of verse 12.

Of all clean birds ye shall eat.

But these are they of which ye shall not eat: the eagle,
and the ossifrage, and the osprey [Deut. 14:11-12].

A few years ago I had a doctor friend, who was a legalist, tell me re-
peatedly that I should not eat pork. One day while we were playing
tennis, I asked him, "Did you ever eat an ossifrage or an osprey?" He
looked at me with a puzzled expression and said that he didn't even
know what they were. I said, "Well, you sure better find out. I might
invite you over someday for dinner and have roast ossifrage. That
would be as bad as eating pork!" He said, "I didn't know that!" So I
told him he had better look it up, and I sent him to this verse and to
Leviticus 11.

RULES CONCERNING THE TITHE

Thou shalt truly tithe all the increase of thy seed, that
the field bringeth forth year by year.

And thou shalt eat before the LORD thy God, in the place
which he shall choose to place his name there, the tithe
of thy corn, of thy wine, and of thine oil, and the first-
lings of thy herds and of thy flocks; that thou mayest
learn to fear the LORD thy God always [Deut. 14:22-23].

God had promised to bless his people in a material way if they would
serve Him. Out of that blessing, they were to tithe for the Lord from
the produce of the land as well as from their flocks. This tithe was to
be eaten before the Lord at the place of the sanctuary. This would be a
special feasting before the Lord.

Then shalt thou turn it into money, and bind up the
money in thine hand, and shalt go unto the place which
the LORD thy God shall choose:

And thou shalt bestow that money for whatsoever thy
soul lusteth after, for oxen, or for sheep, or for wine, or

for strong drink, or for whatsoever thy soul desireth: and thou shalt eat there before the LORD thy God, and thou shalt rejoice, thou, and thine household [Deut. 14:25–26].

If they lived too far from the temple to bring their tithe of produce or livestock, they could turn it into money, then buy their offering to the Lord when they got there.

At the end of three years thou shalt bring forth all the tithe of thine increase the same year, and shalt lay it up within thy gates [Deut. 14:28].

If you will examine the Law carefully, you will find out they actually paid three tithes. That is, 30% of what they made went to the Lord, not just 10%. It seems that the tenth went to the temple immediately, but also there was this tithe at the end of three years.

And the Levite, (because he hath no part nor inheritance with thee,) and the stranger, and the fatherless, and the widow, which are within thy gates, shall come, and shall eat and be satisfied; that the LORD thy God may bless thee in all the work of thine hand which thou doest [Deut. 14:29].

God wanted the Levites, who did the spiritual service for the nation, to be cared for. Also note that God had a concern for the poor.

CHAPTER 15

THEME: God's poverty program; the permanent slave;
the perfect sacrifice is Christ

Today we hear a great deal about poverty programs. Man has devised many programs, but they do not work. God has a poverty program that works.

Then in this chapter there is a section about a permanent slave. And, finally, we find in this chapter a type of the perfect sacrifice which is Christ.

THE SABBATIC YEAR

At the end of every seven years thou shalt make a release [Deut. 15:1].

Every seventh year is a sabbatical year. In that year a release was to be made.

And this is the manner of the release: Every creditor that lendeth aught unto his neighbour shall release it; he shall not exact it of his neighbour, or of his brother; because it is called the LORD's release [Deut. 15:2].

God had already told them that the land was to lie fallow every seventh year. Now we learn about the release on the seventh year. The Israelite could not take a mortgage that went beyond seven years. There could be no foreclosure on a mortgage. When the seventh year came around, money that had been lent or mortgages that had been made were all to be canceled out. This was a great equalizer of the wealth. It gave every man an equal opportunity.

Socialism as it is advocated today does not take into account the fact that man is a sinful creature. If he can get something for nothing, he is not going to work for it; that's for sure. Democracy and capitalism as we have them today allow for extremes. We have the extremely poor who do not work, but we also have the extremely wealthy who do not work. God had a system for Israel which equalized the opportunity so that it was possible for the poor man who really wanted to work to get something for himself. God's system guarded against extreme wealth and extreme poverty.

Of a foreigner thou mayest exact it again: but that which is thine with thy brother thine hand shall release [Deut. 15:3].

This rule held for fellow Israelites. Every seventh year the debt of the poor would be canceled out and they would have an opportunity to start again.

If Israel would observe this carefully, notice what would happen:

Save when there shall be no poor among you; for the LORD shall greatly bless thee in the land which the LORD thy God giveth thee for an inheritance to possess it [Deut. 15:4].

Wherever one goes today, whatever nation one visits, one is impressed by the extremes of poverty and wealth. This is true in Europe, Asia, South America, the United States, wherever one goes. On one side of town there is extreme poverty, and on the other side of town there is extreme wealth. This is the result of the sin of man. One can blame certain individuals, of course, but the basic cause is the sin of man. If man had obeyed God in this respect, there would have been no poor among them; there would have been a balance of wealth.

Until the heart of man is changed, socialism as it is practiced in the communist countries becomes the most frightful dictatorship that is imaginable. Capitalism is still so much better than socialism; but whether a nation has socialism or capitalism, the basic problem is the human heart. God called Israel to obedience. Had they obeyed Him, poverty would have been eliminated. We think that we can eliminate poverty by funding poverty programs. And what happens? We see the worst corruption we have ever seen in this nation. It has become a disgrace. Why? Because of the kind of men we are dealing with. It is not the system that is wrong; it is man that is wrong. There is no use running down one system and promoting another, because until you change man, no system will work. God is dealing with the nitty-gritty here, friends. The basic problem is with the heart of man. What would happen if the wealth of this nation were all divided equally? Well, in ten years the other fellow would have it and I'd be poor again. That is the way it would be because of what is in the heart of man. God makes it very clear that if His system had been used, the problem would have been solved.

> For the LORD thy God blesseth thee, as he promised thee: and thou shalt lend unto many nations, but thou shalt not borrow; and thou shalt reign over many nations, but they shall not reign over thee [Deut. 15:6].

This is a remarkable statement concerning the nation Israel. It is true that many Jewish financiers have become the bankers of the world. The House of Rothschild has financed quite a few nations, by the way. "Thou shalt reign over many nations, but they shall not reign over thee" has not yet been fulfilled. Why? Because Israel has never obeyed God up to the present.

> If there be among you a poor man of one of thy brethren within any of thy gates in thy land which the LORD thy God giveth thee, thou shalt not harden thine heart, nor shut thine hand from thy poor brother:

> But thou shalt open thine hand wide unto him, and shalt surely lend him sufficient for his need, in that which he wanteth [Deut. 15:7–8].

This is a remarkable passage of Scripture. The nation never fully obeyed it, and the Jewish people don't obey it fully today. But have you observed that the little nation of Israel receives gifts from Jewish people all over the world? That nation probably receives more gifts than any other nation ever received. One might think that Christians, certain denominations, certain churches, lead the list in charitable giving, but they do not. Jewish people today are giving millions of dollars to the little nation of Israel. You see, God taught them at the very beginning that they were to take care of their brother. This same principle was also given to the Christian believers—there are certain great, fundamental principles which are eternal truths and which God carries over from one dispensation to another. This is what believers should be doing today. But we are not even in the same league when it comes to helping our brothers. However, I don't think that even Jews come near to what God intended for them when He gave these instructions.

Beware that there be not a thought in thy wicked heart, saying, The seventh year, the year of release, is at hand; and thine eye be evil against thy poor brother, and thou givest him nought; and he cry unto the LORD against thee, and it be sin unto thee [Deut. 15:9].

God warns that they shouldn't rationalize away their responsibility. They could say that since on the seventh year the brother will be out of debt anyway, it will be unnecessary to help him for a year or two. God tells them to go in and help the poor brother right at that very moment.

Thou shalt surely give him, and thine heart shall not be grieved when thou givest unto him: because that for this thing the LORD thy God shall bless thee in all thy works, and in all that thou puttest thine hand unto.

For the poor shall never cease out of the land: therefore I command thee, saying, Thou shalt open thine hand wide unto thy brother, to thy poor, and to thy needy, in thy land [Deut. 15:10–11].

God had told them that if they would obey Him, there would be no poor in the land. But because God knows the human heart, He tells them that there will always be poor people in the land. You remember that the Lord Jesus said the same thing: "The poor always ye have with you . . ." (John 12:8). There will always be poverty because of the heart of man. Candidly, many are lazy; many people are shiftless and have no initiative. On the other hand, those who are able will not normally help the poor. It is not natural for man to do that. It is supernatural for man to share what he has with the less fortunate. Therefore, He commands His people, "Thou shalt open thine hand wide unto thy brother, to thy poor, and to thy needy, in thy land."

Slaves were to be freed on the seventh year.

And when thou sendest him out free from thee, thou shalt not let him go away empty:

Thou shalt furnish him liberally out of thy flock, and out of thy floor, and out of thy winepress: of that wherewith the LORD thy God hath blessed thee thou shalt give unto him [Deut. 15:13–14].

When the slave was freed, he was not to be sent away empty-handed.

THE PERMANENT SLAVE

And it shall be, if he say unto thee, I will not go away from thee; because he loveth thee and thine house, because he is well with thee;

Then thou shalt take an awl and thrust it through his ear unto the door, and he shall be thy servant for ever. And also unto thy maidservant thou shalt do likewise [Deut. 15:16–17].

We saw back in Exodus 21 that a man could sell himself as a slave. If his master had given him a wife—that is, a girl who was his master's slave—when the sabbatical year came, the man could go free. But, perhaps he would choose to stay with his wife and his children and become the permanent slave of his master. Then his ear was to be pierced to signify that he had become a permanent slave.

This is a beautiful picture of the Lord Jesus Christ. He "made himself of no reputation, and took upon him the form of a servant, and was made in the likeness of men: and being found in fashion as a man, he humbled himself, and became obedient unto death, even the death of the cross" (Phil. 2:7–8). Jesus could have gone out free. He owed no debt of sin; He was no sinner. He had no penalty to pay. But He loved us and He gave Himself for us. Just as the servant had his ear thrust through by the awl, so the psalmist says, ". . . mine ears hast thou opened . . ." (Ps. 40:6). The Book of Hebrews takes the same passage from Psalm 40 and says, ". . . but a body hast thou prepared me . . ." (Heb. 10:5). The Lord Jesus took on Himself a human body so that He could be crucified for you and for me. It is one of those remarkable pictures which we find of the Lord Jesus Christ in the Old Testament.

CHAPTER 16

THEME: Three main feasts: Passover, Pentecost, Tabernacles

Israel was given three feasts which all the males were required to attend: Passover, Pentecost (or Weeks), and the Tabernacles.

THE FEAST OF PASSOVER

The Feast of Passover was instituted as a memorial to Israel's deliverance from Egypt and their adoption as Jehovah's nation. The Passover is a festival that laid the foundation of the nation, Israel's birth into a new relationship with God.

> Observe the month of Abib, and keep the passover unto the LORD thy God: for in the month of Abib the LORD thy God brought thee forth out of Egypt by night.
>
> Thou shalt therefore sacrifice the passover unto the LORD thy God, of the flock and the herd, in the place which the LORD shall choose to place his name there [Deut. 16:1–2].

To get the background of the celebration of Passover, turn back to Exodus 12. The children of Israel were in slavery in Egypt. Moses had been chosen by God to lead His people out of Egypt and to the Promised Land. Pharaoh had stubbornly refused to release them, and God revealed His power to Pharaoh by bringing plague after plague upon Egypt. On the fateful night that the final plague was about to descend upon the people, the children of Israel were to express their faith by slaying a lamb, and placing its blood outside the door of the home. Upon seeing the blood, the death angel would pass over the house, which spared the firstborn from death. Because the firstborn died in every home where the blood was absent (including his own), Pharaoh released the children of Israel.

God wanted His people to remember this tremendous deliverance and so instituted the yearly Feast of Passover.

> **Thou mayest not sacrifice the passover within any of thy gates, which the LORD thy God giveth thee:**

> **But at the place which the LORD thy God shall choose to place his name in, there thou shalt sacrifice the passover at even, at the going down of the sun, at the season that thou camest forth out of Egypt.**

> **And thou shalt roast and eat it in the place which the LORD thy God shall choose: and thou shalt turn in the morning, and go unto thy tents.**

> **Six days thou shalt eat unleavened bread: and on the seventh day shall be a solemn assembly to the LORD thy God: thou shalt do no work therein [Deut. 16:5–8].**

That was the Feast of Passover. It was to be observed in one place, which was in Jerusalem. All the males of Israel were to go to Jerusalem at that time.

THE FEAST OF PENTECOST

> **Seven weeks shalt thou number unto thee: begin to number the seven weeks from such time as thou beginnest to put the sickle to the corn.**

> **And thou shalt keep the feast of weeks unto the LORD thy God with a tribute of a freewill offering of thine hand, which thou shalt give unto the LORD thy God, according as the LORD thy God hath blessed thee:**

> **And thou shalt rejoice before the LORD thy God, thou, and thy son, and thy daughter, and thy man-**

> servant, and thy maidservant, and the Levite that is
> within thy gates, and the stranger, and the fatherless,
> and the widow, that are among you, in the place which
> the Lord thy God hath chosen to place his name there
> [Deut. 16:9–11].

Notice that they were to number seven weeks after Passover, which would be forty-nine; then the next day would be the Sabbath, the fiftieth day. Because the Greek word for "fifty" is *pentecoste*, this Feast of Weeks is known as *Pentecost*. It is also called the Feast of Harvest or the Day of First Fruits. It celebrated the first or earliest fruits of the harvest.

THE FEAST OF TABERNACLES

> Thou shalt observe the feast of tabernacles seven days,
> after that thou hast gathered in thy corn and thy wine
> [Deut. 16:13].

This was another feast of rejoicing. It lasted seven days and it, too, was to be kept in the place which the Lord should choose, which was Jerusalem.

> Three times in a year shall all thy males appear before
> the Lord thy God in the place which he shall choose;
> in the feast of unleavened bread, and in the feast of
> weeks, and in the feast of tabernacles: and they shall not
> appear before the Lord empty:
>
> Every man shall give as he is able, according to the
> blessing of the Lord thy God which he hath given thee
> [Deut. 16:16–17].

These are the three feasts which were to be celebrated in Jerusalem, which all males were required to attend. Three times a year they were to travel to Jerusalem to keep these feasts. It was to be a time of rejoicing. Notice they were to come before the Lord with *joy*.

JUDGES IN THE GATES

The chapter concludes with commandments regarding judges.

Judges and officers shalt thou make thee in all thy gates, which the LORD thy God giveth thee, throughout thy tribes: and they shall judge the people with just judgment [Deut. 16:18].

The courthouse in that day was not a building in the center of town or even in a courthouse square. Instead of being in the center of town, it was at the edge of town, at the gate in the wall around the city. The reason for that was that it was the place where all the citizens entered or left the city. It was the gathering place, just as the square is the gathering place in some of our little towns.

Knowing the human heart as God does, He warns against distorting justice, about respect of persons, and about accepting a bribe.

Thou shalt not plant thee a grove of any trees near unto the altar of the LORD thy God, which thou shalt make thee.

Neither shalt thou set thee up any image; which the LORD thy God hateth [Deut. 16:21-22].

A grove was connected with idolatry and with sinful worship in that day. That was the reason they were not to make groves. It was in those groves that the altars and images and idols were made to heathen and pagan gods. You can see that this is very close to the worship of the Druids in Europe. Paganism goes in for that that type of thing, and God is warning His people against it.

CHAPTER 17

THEME: Sundry laws

In chapters 17 and 18 we come to a section which deals with the regulations that would control a king, a priest, and a prophet. These were the three main offices in the nation Israel, in the theocracy which God had set up for these people. God laid down rules for each of these offices.

OFFERING MUST BE WITHOUT DEFECT

Thou shalt not sacrifice unto the Lord thy God any bullock, or sheep, wherein is blemish, or any evilfavouredness: for that is an abomination unto the Lord thy God [Deut. 17:1].

God had said that the firstborn of every creature belongs to Him. Also, that every offering presented to Him was to be without spot or blemish. When you come to the last book of the Old Testament, you will find that Malachi lists the charges which God brought against His people—the sins that brought His judgment down upon them. The number one charge was that they were offering sick animals to God.

Suppose a farmer had a very fine bullock which he had decided to keep. One morning he goes out to his barn lot and finds that this animal is sick. He would say to his boys, "Hustle up, boys; we'll put this bullock in the cart and rush it over to the temple and we'll offer this prize bullock to the Lord." The neighbors would say, "My, my, look at Mr. So-and-So. Isn't he generous! He's giving God that prize bullock." But God, who knows the heart, says, "I will not accept it. Such an offering is absolutely meaningless."

Do you realize that if we as believers were checked out on the way we do business with God, we would be arrested and put in the penitentiary? If we did business with the world or with other individuals in the same manner, we would be put in jail! Each of us should check up on ourselves. How honest are we with God in our financial matters? Don't misunderstand: God is not poor—He owns all the silver and the gold. The cattle on a thousand hills belong to Him; He doesn't need our offering of an old sick cow. Actually, we can't give God anything. Then why does He ask for an offering? He permits us to offer to Him because it is a blessing to our own souls, and we are not blessed when we are beggarly and stingy with God. For instance, we ought to consider what we do for missions. A great many folk today give their castoffs and their secondhand clothes to the missions and to the missionaries. Friends, God does not want our leftovers. He wants our best.

DEATH PENALTY FOR IDOLATERS

If there be found among you, within any of thy gates which the LORD thy God giveth thee, man or woman, that hath wrought wickedness in the sight of the LORD thy God, in transgressing his covenant,

And hath gone and served other gods, and worshipped them, either the sun, or moon, or any of the host of heaven, which I have not commanded;

And it be told thee, and thou hast heard of it, and inquired diligently, and, behold, it be true, and the thing certain, that such abomination is wrought in Israel:

Then shalt thou bring forth that man or that woman, which have committed that wicked thing, unto thy gates, even that man or that woman, and shalt stone them with stones, till they die [Deut. 17:2–5].

This is an absolute law against idolatry. From this and other examples that are given to us, I judge that the penalty for breaking any one of the

Ten Commandments was death. Today we are so "loving" and so "civilized" that we have gotten rid of the death penalty. But the interesting thing is that we have one of the most lawless societies that the world has ever seen. Doesn't it make you wonder if God wasn't right, after all? Stoning was the penalty for idolatry.

You will notice that he mentions idolatry, which was common in the cultures of that day. Greek mythology and the idolatry of the Orient had many gods and goddesses who were associated with the sun, moon, and stars. Apollo was the god of the sun and Artemis the goddess of the moon in the Greek mythology. They worshiped the creature rather than the Creator.

Where did all this begin? I think it began at the Tower of Babel. That Tower of Babel was actually a rallying place for all those who were against God. Why? God had sent a Flood, and now they were going to worship the sun because the sun, according to their reasoning, never sent a flood. The very interesting thing is that they didn't know that the sun is responsible for drawing the water up. The clouds move across the sky and rain falls. The idolatry of that day wasn't very accurate; neither was their science. And maybe the science of our day doesn't have the final word either. A great many people today feel that man's wisdom and knowledge is accurate. Well, we know it has been inaccurate in the past. They worshiped the sun, the moon, and the stars because they thought the heavenly bodies were friendly to them. They worshiped these rather than the Creator who had made them.

At the mouth of two witnesses, or three witnesses, shall he that is worthy of death be put to death; but at the mouth of one witness he shall not be put to death [Deut. 17:6].

Notice how carefully God protects the innocent. A man couldn't rush to the authorities because he didn't like one of his neighbors and accuse his neighbor of worshiping the sun god or Ashtaroth, the Babylonian god, or Baal or Aphrodite or any of the false gods. There had to be two or more witnesses to condemn a man. In our society, one witness could send a man to the gas chamber or the electric chair. I personally think this should not be permitted. God always required two or more witnesses. God is very fair in His dealings.

OBEDIENCE TO AUTHORITY

In the theocracy, they were to refer their cases to the priest or to the judges whom God would put over them. In a theocracy they should never have had a king. We know that later on they asked for a king and God granted their request. Remember Psalm 106:15: "And he gave them their request; but sent leanness into their soul." This was said of their experience in the wilderness, but it is a truth for all time. If God would answer many of our prayers as we pray them, it would be the biggest mistake in the world. God is gracious and many times refuses our requests. He does that for me, and I'm sure He does that for you. However, God yielded to Israel's request for a king. In fact, way back here—before they were even in the land—He was laying down regulations for their king.

If there arise a matter too hard for thee in judgment, between blood and blood, between plea and plea, and between stroke and stroke, being matters of controversy within thy gates: then shalt thou arise, and get thee up into the place which the LORD thy God shall choose [Deut. 17:8].

If two men disagree on an important matter, how is it to be solved when evidence seems to be equally impressive on both sides?

And thou shalt come unto the priests the Levites, and unto the judge that shall be in those days, and inquire; and they shall shew thee the sentence of judgment:

And thou shalt do according to the sentence, which they of that place which the LORD shall choose shall shew thee; and thou shalt observe to do according to all that they inform thee:

> According to the sentence of the law which they shall
> teach thee, and according to the judgment which they
> shall tell thee, thou shalt do: thou shalt not decline for
> the sentence which they shall shew thee, to the right
> hand, nor to the left [Deut. 17:9–11].

Because the Law didn't cover every situation, disagreements were to be taken to the priest. Then the people were to abide by the decision given. Disobedience to the judgment of the priest was to be punished with the death penalty.

The only instance we have recorded of this being used is in Haggai 2:11. I'm sure there were many instances like this. If the Law specifically covered an issue, and dogmatically gave a ruling about it, then, obviously, there was no need to take the matter to the priest. If, however, a matter had to be taken to the priest or the judge for a decision, that decision was final and was to be obeyed.

LAWS CONCERNING A KING

God knows that the time will come when they will demand a king like the other nations had. God says that their king must be an Israelite and not a foreigner.

> But he shall not multiply horses to himself, nor cause
> the people to return to Egypt, to the end that he should
> multiply horses: forasmuch as the LORD hath said unto
> you, Ye shall henceforth return no more that way.
>
> Neither shall he multiply wives to himself, that his heart
> turn not away: neither shall he greatly multiply to him-
> self silver and gold [Deut. 17:16–17].

Here are the rules for the king. It is interesting to note that King Solomon transgressed these rules. First of all, he multiplied horses. When I was at Megiddo, the thing that impressed me there was not so much the battlefield of Armageddon as the ruins of the stables of Solomon.

The stables of Solomon would have made any of the racetracks in this country look like a tenant farmer's barn down in Georgia. And other stables have been excavated at several additional sites. This man, Solomon, went all out in that direction. God warned against this. The raising of horses would get one entangled with Egypt because that was the place where very fine horses were bred.

Then, Solomon transgressed by multiplying wives to himself. God put up warning signs long before Israel ever had a king: "Don't go this way. Be careful." Yet Solomon had many, many wives. It was his wives who turned his heart away from God.

Third, God warned against trying to corner the silver and gold market of that day. Yet that is exactly what Solomon did. David had begun it—but David was collecting silver and gold to build the temple, but Solomon continued collecting silver and gold for himself. This was the undoing of Solomon, and the grievous taxation was the direct cause of the division of Israel as a nation into the northern and southern kingdoms after Solomon's death.

> **And it shall be, when he sitteth upon the throne of his kingdom, that he shall write him a copy of this law in a book out of that which is before the priests the Levites:**
>
> **And it shall be with him, and he shall read therein all the days of his life: that he may learn to fear the LORD his God, to keep all the words of this law and these statutes, to do them:**
>
> **That his heart be not lifted up above his brethren, and that he turn not aside from the commandment, to the right hand, or to the left: to the end that he may prolong his days in his kingdom, he, and his children, in the midst of Israel [Deut. 17:18–20].**

The king was to be a man of the Word of God. He was to have a private copy of the Law of God, and he was to read in it every day of his life.

CHAPTER 18

THEME: *Priest and prophets; the test of a true prophet*

God gives rules regarding the maintenance of the priests. Then there is another warning against idolatrous practices which resort to the satanic powers. This is followed by one of the outstanding sections of the Book of Deuteronomy which deals with prophets, and there is a wonderful prophecy about the Lord Jesus, the Prophet who was to come. The section on prophets concludes with the very interesting and important test for determining true and false prophets.

THE CARE OF THE PRIESTS

The priests the Levites, and all the tribe of Levi, shall have no part nor inheritance with Israel: they shall eat the offerings of the LORD made by fire, and his inheritance.

Therefore shall they have no inheritance among their brethren: the LORD is their inheritance, as he hath said unto them [Deut. 18:1–2].

The priests came from the tribe of Levi. All the Levites were employed in the temple service. They had no land inheritance among the children of Israel, but the Lord was their inheritance. The Lord provided for them in this particular way. It is interesting that God did not mention how a king was to get his salary, but he did give instructions about how a priest was to get his. Yet the preacher's salary is the one thing that is always a touchy issue in the church. God just laid it on the line. He said, "This is what the priests are to receive."

And this shall be the priest's due from the people, from them that offer a sacrifice, whether it be ox or sheep;

> and they shall give unto the priest the shoulder, and the two cheeks, and the maw.
>
> The firstfruit also of thy corn, of thy wine, and of thine oil, and the first of the fleece of thy sheep, shalt thou give him.
>
> For the LORD thy God hath chosen him out of all thy tribes, to stand to minister in the name of the LORD, him and his sons for ever [Deut. 18:3-5].

This is a great principle that God is laying down here. This is still the method God uses to carry on His work in the world. He expects His people to support the people who are giving all of their time in getting out the Word of God to the world. If people started bringing shoulders of beef and of lamb we might have T-bone steaks and lamp chops—of course I do not think He means for us to do it in this same way, but the principle is still true.

> When thou art come into the land which the LORD thy God giveth thee, thou shalt not learn to do after the abominations of those nations.
>
> There shall not be found among you any that maketh his son or his daughter to pass through the fire, or that useth divination, or an observer of times, or an enchanter, or a witch.
>
> Or a charmer, or a consulter with familiar spirits, or a wizard, or a necromancer.
>
> For all that do these things are an abomination unto the LORD: and because of these abominations the LORD thy God doth drive them out from before thee [Deut. 18:9-12].

When these people would go into the land, they were not to resort to the pagan, heathen practices of the people in the land. This warning is repeated in the New Testament. Paul warns ". . . that in the latter times some shall depart from the faith, giving heed to seducing spirits, and doctrines of devils" (1 Tim. 4:1). They will be resorting to the unseen satanic world.

Now let me venture my own judgment, and you can take it for what it is worth. I believe we have now come into that period. As I write, there is a great manifestation of Satan worship. Here, in Southern California, there are churches of Satan where he is actually worshiped. In Hawaii, I saw a group of young people falling down before a picture of Krishna, which is nothing in the world but satanic worship. Some people pass this off as a fad because it is a tendency of human nature to go after fads—especially in America. However, there is a great deal of reality in Satan worship. It is not a group of stupid people, nor is it only the uneducated who are indulging in this sort of thing. There must be reality in it and, since Satan is real, I believe there is a certain amount of reality in it. But God warns against this. He says it is an abomination unto Him.

I want to add this because someone needs to say it today. There is a danger in playing with astrology. Remember that in the previous chapter we read the condemnation of the worship of sun, moon, and stars. There are a great many people today who are placing more emphasis on astrology than they are on the Bible. Stores and magazine racks are loaded with material on astrology. The media is promoting it. We see it everywhere we turn. My friend, astrology is an abomination unto the Lord. Don't find fault with me for saying this. It is God who calls it an abomination. Why is it an abomination? It takes people away from the living and true God. It plunges them into darkness and demonism. There is reality in the world of demons. There are fallen angels and a spirit world. This thing is real, and today people are intrigued with it. They use drugs and every other means they can think of to try to make contact with this unseen world. And the satanic world is very glad to make contact with them. A child of God should let this thing alone. Anyone who turns in that direction has a weak faith and is not really trusting Christ as Savior. He is turning away from the Holy Spirit and the Word of God. God has given warnings about this sort of thing. His warnings have happened to be very accurate in the past. His batting average, friends, is excellent—He hasn't missed yet. He hits a home run every time, and I am going to go along with Him.

> Thou shalt be perfect with the LORD thy God.

> For these nations, which thou shalt possess, hearkened unto observers of times, and unto diviners: but as for thee, the LORD thy God hath not suffered thee so to do [Deut. 18:13–14].

These nations in the land were judged and would be removed from the land because of this very thing. Israel has been called to be a witness to the true and living God.

PROMISE OF THE COMING MESSIAH

> The LORD thy God will raise up unto thee a Prophet from the midst of thee, of thy brethren, like unto me; unto him ye shall hearken:

> According to all that thou desiredst of the LORD thy God in Horeb in the day of the assembly, saying, Let me not hear again the voice of the LORD my God, neither let me see this great fire any more, that I die not.

> And the LORD said unto me, They have well spoken that which they have spoken [Deut. 18:15–17].

The children of Israel were to listen to God's prophets. Why? Because they were telling them the truth. That was the basic reason. But the second reason was to prepare them to listen to the final messenger, the final Prophet, the Lord Jesus Christ.

Some people still ask why God does not reveal Himself today. Friend, in the person of the Lord Jesus Christ, God put the period at the end of the sentence. God wrote *finis* at the end of the book. He has nothing more to say to the world than He has said in Jesus Christ. We are to hear *Him*. We are to hearken unto *Him*. At the Transfiguration, God the Father said, "This is my beloved Son, in whom I am well pleased; hear ye him" (Matt. 17:5). Listen to Him. He has the final Word. For believers today the Lord Jesus Christ is God's ultimate, God's full, God's final revelation to man. This is what Moses is saying way back here in Deuteronomy.

> **I will raise them up a Prophet from among their brethren, like unto thee, and will put my words in his mouth; and he shall speak unto them all that I shall command him.**
>
> **And it shall come to pass, that whosoever will not hearken unto my words which he shall speak in my name, I will require it of him [Deut. 18:18–19].**

You will recall that the Lord Jesus said again and again that the words He spoke were not His own but the Father's. For instance, in John 5:30, and several times in John 6, the Lord Jesus says that He came not to do His own will but to do the will of the Father. After the Lord's earthly ministry was finished, he prayed in that great high priestly prayer, where He is turning in His final report to the Father, ". . . I have finished the work which thou gavest me to do. . . . For I have given unto them the words which thou gavest me . . ." (John 17:4, 8). If God were to speak out of heaven at this very moment, He would not say anything that He had not already said. He would just repeat Himself, because all He intends to say to you and to me is in the person of Christ.

That is the reason we are to let astrology alone. It is the tendency of human nature to want to explore the unknown, to know about the future. There is an insatiable desire to probe the mysterious. There is some of the spirit of Columbus in all of us. Right now we are exploring space and the depths of the oceans. We like to reach out into new areas. Not only do we do this in space, but man also likes to reach out in time. He wants to know about that mysterious future. What is beyond tomorrow? What does the future hold? All would like to know that, would they not? People are anxious about the future. There is always the question: What about tomorrow? The future is a closed door. Memory can take you back into the past, but there is no vehicle to take you into the future. Written in the door of the future are the words, "Keep Out!" Today was tomorrow only yesterday. Man is limited as to time and also space.

To satisfy this insatiable longing, there arose among the heathen spiritualists, necromancers, and diviners. God warned His people against it. This was connected with idolatry and was satanic in origin. Could they tell the future? Yes, there was a certain degree of accuracy. The Greeks used the Oracle of Delphi and, apparently, got a certain amount of accurate information there—but it was satanic. They say that Hitler resorted to some type of fortune-teller. I understand in Washington today, fortune-tellers do a land-office business. The classified ads in any city will show you that there are many fortune-tellers making a very fine living by speaking of the future.

Now the future is an area in which man has never been given dominion. God alone can predict the future, and it belongs to Him. A unique character of the Word of God is that it moves beyond the present. The greatest proof to me that the Bible is the Word of God is the fulfillment of prophecy. One-fourth of the entire Bible was prophecy at the time it was written, and a large portion of that has already been fulfilled. God has recorded prophecies concerning cities and nations and great world empires. Under such circumstances, there would arise false prophets, as there are today. They wanted the status and the position that belonged to the true prophet of God. How could Israel protect themselves from the false prophets? God lays down a test by which they could be certain a man was either a true prophet of God or a phony.

TEST FOR DETERMINING TRUE
AND FALSE PROPHETS

There were false prophets among the people; that's quite evident. Unfortunately, Israel would not apply God's rules by which they could identify them. We find this passage in Jeremiah 14:14: "Then the LORD said unto me, The prophets prophesy lies in my name: I sent them not, neither have I commanded them, neither spake unto them: they prophesy unto you a false vision and divination, and a thing of nought, and the deceit of their heart." It was easy enough for a false prophet to speak of the coming Kingdom—centuries in the future. The prophet Jeremiah spoke of the future. Today we can know because a great deal of Jeremiah's prophecy has been fulfilled, but how could people know at the time it was spoken? Well, God put down a very accurate test. Listen to Him:

> **But the prophet, which shall presume to speak a word in my name, which I have not commanded him to speak, or that shall speak in the name of other gods, even that prophet shall die.**

> **And if thou say in thine heart, How shall we know the word which the LORD hath not spoken?**

> **When a prophet speaketh in the name of the LORD, if the thing follow not, nor come to pass, that is the thing which the LORD hath not spoken, but the prophet hath spoken it presumptuously: thou shalt not be afraid of him [Deut. 18:20–22].**

Let us take time to look at this for a moment. Isaiah is a prophet of God, a true prophet of God. How do we know? He prophesied that a virgin would conceive and bring forth a son. He clearly marked out the coming of the Lord Jesus, His birth, His life, His death. Suppose someone had asked Isaiah when all this would take place. He would have answered that he was not quite sure but that it could be hundreds of years. (Actually, it was seven hundred years.) Well, that crowd would laugh and say they would never be around to know whether he was telling the truth or not. The test of the prophets was that they had to give a prediction about a local situation that would come to pass right away, and they had to be *completely accurate*. They couldn't miss in any point of their predictions. Any inaccuracy at all would immediately disqualify them as a true prophet of God.

Now let us look at Isaiah again. He prophesied the virgin birth, and we today can look back 1900 years to the fulfillment of that and know that he was accurate. But how could the people in his day know that? They could know because Isaiah went to the king, Hezekiah, with a prophecy concerning a local current event. There was a great Assyrian army of trigger-happy soldiers surrounding the city, but Isaiah said that not one arrow would enter the city. Those Assyrians had conquered other nations and they were there to conquer Jerusalem and to carry Israel into captivity. Isaiah told them what God had said about it:

"Therefore thus saith the LORD concerning the king of Assyria. He shall not come into this city, nor shoot an arrow there, nor come before it with shields, nor cast a bank against it. By the way that he came, by the same shall he return, and shall not come into this city, said the LORD" (Isa. 37:33–34).

All of those fellows in the Assyrian army had bows and arrows. You'd think that just one of them might let an arrow fly over the wall just to see if he could hit someone. Now if one arrow was shot into the city, Isaiah would lose his job as a true prophet of God. He would be out of business. That was one of the tests which Isaiah passed. There were others where Isaiah spoke to a local situation, and it came to pass just as he had said. The true prophet had to be correct 100 percent of the time.

Now what about today? This test would disqualify everyone on the contemporary scene who claims to be a prophet by predicting the future. I grant you that some of them sometimes hit the nail right on the head, but more often they miss the nail altogether. You don't hear of their misses; you only hear of their accurate guesses. I could give many instances of false prophecies. We have folk predicting the end of the world on a certain date, the Rapture of the church on a certain date, calamities that will come to a particular section of the country on a specific date, and a host of other things. If we applied God's test to these self-acclaimed prophets, they would be out of business in short order. A true prophet must be accurate in every detail every time.

But do you know that there are no warnings about false prophets for the church today? Why? Because there is no more prophecy to be

CHAPTER 19

THEME: Cities of refuge; extent of the land and the extremity of the Law

The provision of cities of refuge, the protection of property rights, and the severity of the Law reveal again God's concern for the innocent person.

CITIES OF REFUGE

In the Book of Numbers, chapter 35, we learn that the Levites were to set up three such cities on the east side of Jordan and three on the west side of Jordan.

> Thou shalt separate three cities for thee in the midst of thy land, which the LORD thy God giveth thee to possess it.
>
> Thou shalt prepare thee a way, and divide the coasts of thy land, which the LORD thy God giveth thee to inherit, into three parts, that every slayer may flee thither.
>
> And this is the case of the slayer, which shall flee thither, that he may live: Whoso killeth his neighbour ignorantly, whom he hated not in time past [Deut. 19:2–4].

A man who had unwittingly killed a person could flee to a city of refuge. This would save him from mob action or from the action of some hotheaded relative who might be emotionally wrought up at the time. In a city of refuge he would be protected until a fair trial could be held.

God makes it perfectly clear that the cities of refuge were to be protection for the innocent man. He gives an example of what he means by an accidental killing.

> As when a man goeth into the wood with his neighbour
> to hew wood, and his hand fetcheth a stroke with the
> axe to cut down the tree, and the head slippeth from the
> helve, and lighteth upon his neighbour, that he die; he
> shall flee unto one of those cities, and live:

> Lest the avenger of the blood pursue the slayer, while his
> heart is hot, and overtake him, because the way is long,
> and slay him; whereas he was not worthy of death, inas-
> much as he hated him not in time past [Deut. 19:5–6].

The Lord is specific that the cities of refuge are not to be protection for
those guilty of murder.

> But if any man hate his neighbour, and lie in wait for
> him, and rise up against him, and smite him mortally
> that he die, and fleeth into one of these cities:

> Then the elders of his city shall send and fetch him
> thence, and deliver him into the hand of the avenger of
> blood, that he may die [Deut. 19:11–12].

PROTECTION OF PROPERTY

> Thou shalt not remove thy neighbour's landmark,
> which they of old time have set in thine inheritance,
> which thou shalt inherit in the land that the LORD thy
> God giveth thee to possess it [Deut. 19:14].

Here is the fact that landmarks were sacred. This was a protection of
human property and establishes the rights to property.

> One witness shall not rise up against a man for any in-
> iquity, or for any sin, in any sin that he sinneth: at the
> mouth of two witnesses, or at the mouth of three wit-
> nesses, shall the matter be established [Deut. 19:15].

This passage reveals to us the awesomeness of the Law. The demands of the Law were terrible, and under no circumstances was one witness sufficient. Anyone today who says that he wants to live under law should really find out what it is.

If a false witness should arise, then the accused and the accuser were to stand before the Lord, represented by the priests and the judges. If the judges decided that the witness was false, then whatever he wanted to have done to the accused was the punishment which would be given to him. In that way, evil was to be removed from the nation (vv. 16–20).

And thine eye shall not pity; but life shall go for life, eye for eye, tooth for tooth, hand for hand, foot for foot [Deut. 19:21].

That is law, friends. There is no mercy in law. I thank God today that the Lord is not judging me on the basis of law. He saves me by grace. If he were saving me by law, I would be lost forever, because I could never, never measure up to the requirements of the Law. Law is *law*—we have developed such a careless attitude about it today—but God *enforces* His Law. It was eye for eye, tooth for tooth. How I thank God that Jesus Christ paid the penalty of the Law so that there is pardon for sinners. The throne of God has become a mercy seat because Christ died and His blood has been sprinkled there—and that's the blood of the covenant. God saves us by His grace. We have not kept the Law; we have broken it. We are all guilty before God. Christ paid the penalty; so the requirements of the Law have been fulfilled. Now God is free to save sinners by His marvelous, infinite, wonderful grace.

CHAPTER 20

THEME: Laws regulating warfare

This Book of Deuteronomy is a very practical book. It touches life where we live it today. Although these laws were given to Israel, there are certain basic principles here which would contribute to the happiness and the welfare of mankind if they were incorporated into the laws of modern nations. I'm convinced that the men who originally drew up our constitution were men who were Bible-oriented. The problem today is that we have a society made up of people who are entirely ignorant of the Bible, and lawmakers who are actually stupid as far as the Word of God is concerned. The blunders they make in their policies are enough to cause us to weep and howl—all because they are so far from God and not following Him at all. This Book of Deuteronomy covers problems which Washington has been trying to solve in its own way. Our lawmakers have been wrestling with these problems for years.

They have dealt with the problem of our young men for service in the armed forces. They are troubled to know what should be the conditions on which a man should serve or not serve. Israel had these same problems. God put down certain very basic rules that would prevent a man from going to war. Very candidly, I am of the opinion that if our government had paid attention to God's Law relative to this, we wouldn't be in the mess we are in today.

> **When thou goest out to battle against thine enemies and seest horses, and chariots, and a people more than thou, be not afraid of them: for the LORD thy God is with thee, which brought thee up out of the land of Egypt [Deut. 20:1].**

Here was something that was important for Israel, and I believe it is important for us today. We see little mottos which read, "Make love, not war." That may sound good, but like so many little mottos, it is absolutely meaningless. Because we are living in a sinful world where the heart of man is desperately wicked, there are times to make war. There are times when we need to protect ourselves. There are wars in which God is on one side. Frankly, the important question any nation should consider—and certainly a so-called civilized and Christian nation—is whether this is a war that God is in. If He isn't in it, then we shouldn't be in it either.

> **And it shall be, when ye are come nigh unto the battle, that the priest shall approach and speak unto the people.**

> **And shall say unto them, Hear, O Israel, ye approach this day unto battle against your enemies: let not your hearts faint, fear not, and do not tremble, neither be ye terrified because of them;**

> **For the LORD your God is he that goeth with you, to fight for you against your enemies, to save you [Deut. 20:2–4].**

This is something that is very important in warfare. Make sure that you are on God's side. God commanded them to war against these nations and promised that He would be with them.

Now God puts down four conditions, or four excuses, which would keep a man from going to battle.

> **And the officers shall speak unto the people, saying, What man is there that hath built a new house, and hath not dedicated it? let him go and return to his house, lest he die in the battle, and another man dedicate it [Deut. 20:5].**

If a man has built a new home and has not had the opportunity to live in it, he was not to go into battle. Why not? Because his heart, naturally, would be in that new home. He had set his heart and his affection on it. He wanted to live in that new home, and he is to be given the opportunity to live in it.

> **And what man is he that hath planted a vineyard, and hath not yet eaten of it? let him also go and return unto his house, lest he die in the battle, and another man eat of it [Deut. 20:6].**

These people were agrarian; they were farmers. Here is a man who has just gotten started in business; he had just planted a vineyard. Because he hasn't had the opportunity to eat a grape off it yet, he is not to go to battle. His heart is in his vineyard; his interest is there. He is to stay until he gets to eat of it, until he gets established. Otherwise he might be killed in battle, and another man would reap the fruit of his labors. This is quite interesting, is it not?

> **And what man is there that hath betrothed a wife, and hath not taken her? let him go and return unto his house, lest he die in the battle, and another man take her [Deut. 20:7].**

Here is a young man who is engaged to a girl and he gets drafted. He is not to be taken. He is in love with that girl, he wants to marry her. Let him stay home, and let him marry the girl. That is where his heart is, and he is not to go to battle.

Now here is the fourth excuse:

> **And the officers shall speak further unto the people, and they shall say, What man is there that is fearful and fainthearted? let him go and return unto his house, lest his brethren's heart faint as well as his heart [Deut. 20:8].**

There might be a man who very frankly says, "I am a coward. I am afraid to fight, and I don't want to fight." So here are four good reasons for a man not to go to war. I could not have used the first three reasons, but that last one I could have used. If a man was afraid, faint-hearted, fearful, he was not to go. I believe I would have turned and gone home.

This law was applied to Gideon's army. You may remember that Gideon started out with quite an army—32,000 men who rallied to him to free their nation from the oppression of the Midianites who had actually impoverished them. Then the Lord told him he had too many soldiers, and that whoever was fearful and afraid could go home! When that word went out, 22,000 men picked up their gear and went home! Then God told Gideon that he still had too many men. How were they separated? They came to a stream and some of the men got down on all fours to drink. There were others who lapped up the water like a dog and were all set to go. They were eager to get to the enemy and get the job done. They wanted to free and save their nation. So they were the ones who went to battle, and the others were sent home.

In America we have had problems with our young men dodging the draft and burning their draft cards. I have great sympathy with many of these young men, but I wish instead of trying to blame the government and blame everybody else, they would just come out and say they are afraid to go fight. That is a good reason. That would have kept me out of the battle, I can assure you of that. I don't mind admitting I'm a coward. For example, because I had to work my way through high school and college, and support my mother, I could never have proven that I was a good enough football player to earn a scholarship. But I played a little and enjoyed it. I remember how I felt just before that kickoff. When the whistle was blown—I played the backfield—standing way back there, my knees would buckle. There were times when I'd actually go down on one knee, I was so scared. But the minute I got the ball and I was hit, from then on I was all right. But I would never have made it in combat on the battlefield, I can assure you!

God says here that He wants His people to know two things before they go to war. First of all, they must be on His side. They must be fighting for what is right and know that God is with them. Secondly, they must be enthusiastic about it. There is a time when one should fight for his country, and there is a place for the flag and for patriotism. The way things are carried out by our politicians actually encourages this motley mob who burn their draft cards. But the way God does it is very wise. He had a marvelous arrangement for His people, even in time of war.

> **When thou comest nigh unto a city to fight against it, then proclaim peace unto it.**
>
> **And it shall be, if it makes thee answer of peace, and open unto thee, then it shall be, that all the people that is found therein shall be tributaries unto thee, and they shall serve thee.**
>
> **And if it will make no peace with thee, but will make war against thee, then thou shalt besiege it [Deut. 20:10–12].**

Here is another great principle which is laid down. You may remember that General Douglas MacArthur did not believe in fighting a war which we did not intend to win. This kind of compromise is the curse of our nation today, and we do it with a phony piousness. This has pervaded our churches, and today it is in our government. We pretend to be the great big wonderful brother. MacArthur warned, in his day, not to fight a land war in Asia. But if we fight in a war, we are to fight to win—that is the purpose of it. And that is exactly what God says. We have no business to fight a war unless we are fighting to win it.

God has put down some very good principles here, friends, but today we have departed far from them.

CHAPTER 21

THEME: Laws regarding murder, marriage, and delinquent sons

This chapter concludes the section concerning religious and national regulations which began with chapter 8. We find here interesting and remarkable laws regulating many different aspects of the life of Israel.

> If one be found slain in the land which the LORD thy God giveth thee to possess it, lying in the field, and it be not known who hath slain him:
>
> Then thy elders and thy judges shall come forth, and they shall measure unto the cities which are round about him that is slain:
>
> And it shall be, that the city which is next unto the slain man, even the elders of that city shall take an heifer, which hath not been wrought with, and which hath not drawn in the yoke:
>
> And the elders of that city shall bring down the heifer unto a rough valley, which is neither eared nor sown, and shall strike off the heifer's neck there in the valley [Deut. 21:1–4].

If a man has obviously been murdered and his body is found, the officials of the city are to measure to find the closest city. Then that city is held responsible for the murder. It may not be that he was slain in the city, but the city is still held responsible.

This is what they are to do:

> And the priests the sons of Levi shall come near; for them the LORD thy God hath chosen to minister unto

him, and to bless in the name of the LORD; and by their word shall every controversy and every stroke be tried:

And all the elders of that city, that are next unto the slain man, shall wash their hands over the heifer that is beheaded in the valley:

And they shall answer and say, Our hands have not shed this blood, neither have our eyes seen it.

Be merciful, O LORD, unto thy people Israel, whom thou hast redeemed, and lay not innocent blood unto thy people of Israel's charge. And the blood shall be forgiven them.

So shalt thou put away the guilt of innocent blood from among you, when thou shalt do that which is right in the sight of the LORD [Deut. 21:5-9].

There is a basic truth taught in this procedure. When a crime takes place in a city, the inhabitants of that city have a certain responsibility. This is my reason for believing that ultimately there will have to be a demand made by concerned citizens that laws be enforced to get rid of the crimes that are taking place. God holds a community responsible. Even if the murder was not committed in the city, the city still is responsible. The elders of that city were to come and ask for forgiveness for the city, and forgiveness would be granted them.

In America I wonder if there ever is even a suggestion that we ask God for forgiveness for our many crimes and the many things happening in our land. It is one thing to say that things are terrible, things are awful. It is another thing to go to God and say, "Oh, God, forgive us as a nation. God, forgive us for our sins today."

Do you know that Christ was murdered outside a city? Yes, He was. But His death could save His murderers. I think the Roman centurion who had charge of His crucifixion is one of the men who was saved.

Verses 10–17 give the law regulating marriage with a woman who was captured in warfare. Also there is the legal protection of the rights of the firstborn in the case of dual marriage where one wife was loved and the one was hated. We have seen this illustrated in the life of Jacob.

> **If a man have a stubborn and rebellious son, which will not obey the voice of his father, or the voice of his mother, and that, when they have chastened him, will not hearken unto them:**
>
> **Then shall his father and his mother lay hold on him, and bring him out unto the elders of his city, and unto the gate of his place;**
>
> **And they shall say unto the elders of his city, This our son is stubborn and rebellious, he will not obey our voice; he is a glutton, and a drunkard.**
>
> **And all the men of his city shall stone him with stones, and he die: so shalt thou put evil away from among you; and all Israel shall hear, and fear [Deut. 21:18–21].**

Here is the law concerning the "prodigal son." We can understand how our Lord shocked the crowd listening to Him when He told them the parable of the prodigal son. When that boy came home, the listening crowd would expect that he would be stoned. Imagine their surprise when our Lord said that the father went out with open arms to meet the boy. They had expected the boy to get what he justly deserved. He had been a disgrace. He deserved to die. But what does the father do? He puts his arms around the boy and kisses him. He says, ". . . let us eat, and be merry: for this my son was dead, and is alive again; he was lost, and is found" (Luke 15:23–24).

Friends, aren't you glad that we are not under law today? When we come to God, and we confess our sins, "He is faithful and just to forgive us our sins, and to cleanse us from all unrighteousness" (1 John 1:9). Instead of judgment, there is mercy for us. How wonderful and how merciful God is to accept us and receive us when we come to Him!

Now we have the strange case of one being hanged on a tree.

And if a man have committed a sin worthy of death, and he be to be put to death, and thou hang him on a tree:

His body shall not remain all night upon the tree, but thou shalt in any wise bury him that day; (for he that is hanged is accursed of God;) that thy land be not defiled, which the LORD thy God giveth thee for an inheritance [Deut. 21:22–23].

A criminal who was executed by hanging was not to remain on the tree all night. This was because everyone who hangs on a tree is accursed. It seems strange to us that this law is mentioned here. The form of capital punishment which was used in Israel was stoning. Apparently Israel did not use hanging as a form of capital punishment. So what this really means is that a person who was put to death by stoning was then hung on a tree. This applies to criminals of the worst type, to let it be seen that he had died for his terrible crime. It would be a warning to others. The body was to be taken down from the tree by nightfall and buried. The reason was that the criminal was accursed of God.

Probably Moses did not realize, and certainly the children of Israel did not realize, the full significance of this law. In Galatians 3:13, Paul picks up this statement in the law and applies it to Christ. "Christ hath redeemed us from the curse of the law, being made a curse for us: for it is written, Cursed is every one that hangeth on a tree." In the time when our Lord Jesus lived on earth, He was delivered into the hands of the Romans for execution. Because Rome was in control of the land, the death penalty could only be executed by Rome. Our Lord was crucified on a Roman cross, sometimes called a tree. Now Paul picks that up and says that when Christ was hanging there on the tree, He was taking our sins and was accursed of God in that condition. Because of what He had done? No. He became a curse for us to redeem us from the curse of sin. He redeemed us from the penalty of sin, and He has bought our pardon. Why? Because He was made a curse for us.

I get weary of people arguing about whether the Romans or the Jews were to blame for the death of the Lord Jesus. Actually you and I were responsible for His death. Christ was made a curse for us. This is the thing He did for us on the Cross, which makes us responsible for His death.

CHAPTER 22

THEME: Miscellaneous laws concerning brother relationships, mixtures, and marriage

This chapter brings us to another division of the Book of Deuteronomy. We have seen the repetition and interpretation of the Ten Commandments in chapters 5—7. Then there are the religious and national regulations in chapters 8—21. Now we come to regulations for domestic and personal relations in chapters 22—26. God directed many of these laws to the nation; now He gets right down to the nitty-gritty where the people live with laws relative to their domestic and their personal relations.

BROTHER RELATIONSHIPS

Thou shalt not see thy brother's ox or his sheep go astray, and hide thyself from them: thou shalt in any case bring them again unto thy brother.

And if thy brother be not nigh unto thee, or if thou know him not, then thou shalt bring it unto thine own house, and it shall be with thee until thy brother seek after it, and thou shalt restore it to him again [Deut. 22:1–2].

In my day we have heard a great deal about a good neighbor policy, and we see that God had a good neighbor policy for His people in that day. I remember during Franklin Roosevelt's administration when he came out with the "good neighbor policy," all the pundits and reporters acclaimed it as something brand new. They hailed Roosevelt as a sort of messiah and thought he had come up with something wonderful. May I say to you that the good neighbor policy is as old as Moses—actually much older than Moses. It goes back to the very throne of God in eternity. He is the One who says we are to adopt a good neighbor policy, and it is to be demonstrated in our everyday life.

Thou shalt not see thy brother's ass or his ox fall down by the way, and hide thyself from them: thou shalt surely help him to lift them up again [Deut. 22:4].

They were not to assume a nonchalant attitude toward the neighbor, nor were they to pass by as if the neighbor's problem were none of their business. They were to extend their help to the neighbor.

DRESS CODE

The woman shall not wear that which pertaineth unto a man, neither shall man put on a woman's garment: for all that do so are abomination unto the LORD thy God [Deut. 22:5].

Someone will say this does not apply to us today because we are not under the Law. That is true. However, all these laws which we are studying do lay down certain principles which we do well to notice. I may be out of step with the times, but I believe it is still true today that a woman looks better dressed as a woman, and a man looks better dressed as a man.

As my wife and I were driving in San Francisco, we were behind a little Volkswagen. I remarked that the wife was driving and the man was sitting next to her, and she was driving pretty fast. When they were going up a hill, they couldn't maintain their speed, so I passed them. Do you know that I was wrong? The man was driving and the woman was sitting beside him. That man looked a woman, and the woman looked like a man. Frankly, I don't see the benefit of that.

God created us male and female. God is saying here that a man ought to look like a man, and a woman ought to look like a woman. We are having a great deal of trouble today because the sexes are trying to look alike and are trying to act alike. I personally feel that womanhood is paying an awful price for demanding equal rights. Men would like to treat women as women, and that means men would like to elevate them, and give them more than equal rights.

PROTECTION FOR BIRDS

If a bird's nest chance to be before thee in the way in any tree, or on the ground, whether they be young ones, or eggs, and the dam sitting upon the young, or upon the eggs, thou shalt not take the dam with the young:

But thou shalt in any wise let the dam go, and take the young to thee; that it may be well with thee, and that thou mayest prolong thy days [Deut. 22:6-7].

It is a wonderful thing to see that God is concerned for birds. Remember the Lord Jesus said that not even a single sparrow falls without the Father's knowledge (Matt. 10:29). Actually, the language has the thought that a sparrow always falls into the lap of the Father. Just a bird—yet the Father is concerned about it! The Lord Jesus said, "Fear ye not therefore, ye are of more value than many sparrows" (Matt. 10:31). How wonderful that is. If the Father is concerned about a sparrow, He is also concerned and knows all about you.

BUILDING CODE

When thou buildest a new house, then thou shalt make a battlement for thy roof, that thou bring no blood upon thine house, if any man fall from thence [Deut. 22:8].

One must understand that the roof of the house in that day in Israel served as the front porch, the patio, the deck, whatever you wish to call it. It was the place where the family went to sit in the cool of the evening. Now God says that the area is to be protected. There was to be a railing around it so little children would not fall off and so that people would not step off the roof in the darkness.

Do you know that it is only in recent years that our nation has had building codes to protect people? God is not behind the times as a great many people seem to think He is. God has a concern about the way people build their homes. He is interested in that.

He wants your home to be dedicated to Him, and He wants that home to be a safe place. Do you have a railing around your home? Do you protect your children from the things of this world? Many parents let their children move from the home and do not even know where the children are. Many children have gone out to live on the street or in communes. The railing, the protection, is not there as it should be in the modern home.

MIXTURES

Thou shalt not sow thy vineyard with divers seeds: lest the fruit of thy seed which thou hast sown, and the fruit of thy vineyard, be defiled.

Thou shalt not plow with an ox and ass together [Deut. 22:9–10].

This sounds to me like a humorous thing which the Lord is saying here. Actually I saw this done over in Israel. In fact, I have a slide that I took showing an Arab plowing with an ox and an ass yoked together. So they do this over there even today. God says that Israel should not plow that way. Someone may ask, "What is wrong with that?" Well, an ox is an ox and an ass is an ass, and they do not go together. They don't walk together—their gait is different, and they do not pull together.

Have you noticed that the Lord does not like mixtures? The same thing is true in marriage. God does not want a mixture of the saved and the unsaved. Unfortunately, I have seen quite a few marriages that reminded me of an ox and an ass yoked together—a Christian girl marries an unsaved fellow, or vice versa.

Thou shalt not wear a garment of divers sorts, as of woolen and linen together [Deut. 22:11].

Do you know what happens with a mixture like that? When you wash it, the wool will shrink but the linen will not. Then you have a real problem.

Thou shalt make thee fringes upon the four quarters of thy vesture, wherewith thou coverest thyself [Deut. 22:12].

That fringe was most generally blue. We know it was blue on the garment of the high priest. The fringe was a reminder of their relationship to God. Later the fringes became distinct badges of Judaism.

God warns against mixtures. The child of God cannot mix with the world. I hear Christians say that they go the way of the world in order to reach the people of the world. I have news for you. That is not the way to reach them. If you ever hear of anybody being reached because a Christian went the way of the world, let me know. The seeds were not to be mixed. The ox and the ass were not to try to work together. The wool and the linen were not to be mixed. The Christian is not to mix with the world, my friend.

MARRIAGE

If any man take a wife, and go in unto her, and hate her,

And give occasions of speech against her, and bring up an evil name upon her, and say, I took this woman, and when I came to her, I found her not a maid:

Then shall the father of the damsel, and her mother, take and bring forth the tokens of the damsel's virginity unto the elders of the city in the gate [Deut. 22:13–15].

Here was a law to protect the innocent wife, and it was to keep a wife from being falsely charged. This protected a wife from a godless and hateful husband. It was a way we do not have today, but God had made an arrangement to protect a wife under such circumstances.

But if this thing be true, and the tokens of virginity be not found for the damsel:

Then they shall bring out the damsel to the door of her father's house, and the men of her city shall stone her with stones that she die: because she hath wrought folly in Israel, to play the whore in her father's house: so shalt thou put evil away from among you [Deut. 22:20–21].

Suppose the woman was guilty. Then she was to be stoned.

Today people talk about the "new" morality and consider sex apart from marriage a great step forward. God gave a standard of morality to His people, Israel. God-given morality has always been a blessing to any nation. Any nation that has broken over at this point has gone down. When I think of this, and when I think of the condition of my country, I weep. Under God's law to Israel, a person guilty of adultery was stoned to death, whether man or woman. If we did that here in Southern California, there would be so many rock piles it would be impossible to drive a car through this part of the country.

God honors marriage and God honors sexual purity. Adultery in Israel was to be punished by stoning. This tells us how God feels about adultery, friends. Remember that God's love for His people is expressed in His Law. This law regarding the protection of the sanctity of marriage is a very fine example of His love and concern for the human family.

CHAPTER 23

THEME: The world, the flesh, and the devil

Chapter 23 continues this very interesting section regarding regulations for domestic and personal relationships. The world, the flesh, and the devil are the three enemies a believer contends with daily, even hourly, and moment by moment.

We are living in a day when very plain language is being used—in fact, vulgar language. God in His Word also uses very plain language, but it is by no means vulgar. Where the Bible deals with very personal issues, that section is generally avoided. However, I do not think we should avoid it, as it holds very practical spiritual lessons for us.

He that is wounded in the stones, or hath his privy member cut off, shall not enter into the congregation of the LORD [Deut. 23:1].

This is a most unusual law, is it not? What is God trying to teach us here? I believe that this would correspond to asceticism, and God condemns it.

During the Middle Ages, men saw the corruption in Europe and in Asia and in North Africa, and they turned from the things of the world to become ascetics. They retired to monasteries to get away from the world. Very candidly, one probably couldn't blame them for doing it at that time. But this is an extreme and God warns against it.

In Protestantism one can find that same type of legalism today. There are those who feel they are living the "separated life." Yet I have never found one of those folk to be a joyful person. As a matter of fact, I have found some of them to be dangerous people. They act very pious and seem very shocked when anything that is worldly is mentioned before them. I have found that those same people can be the meanest gossips, and that they are not always honorable in their business relations. I have had a very bitter experience in my own life with a little group of "separated Christians" who were totally, absolutely dishonest. I believe God is warning against asceticism. He does not accept that kind of thing.

A bastard shall not enter into the congregation of the LORD; even to his tenth generation shall he not enter into the congregation of the LORD [Deut. 23:2].

God uses some pretty strong language here. An illegitimate child could not enter the congregation of the Lord. What does that mean for us today?

You must be born again to be a child of God. There are a lot of people today who say, "I am a child of the King," but they are not a child of the King. They are illegitimate. One can be religious and not be born again. Such a one is not a child of God at all. God makes that very clear. Nicodemus was a Pharisee, a very religious man, a spiritual ruler of the people, a man who wore his phylacteries. Yet that man was illegitimate, and our Lord said to him that he must be born again. Our Lord almost rudely interrupted him to make that clear to him (John 3:3).

As I hold many meetings all over this country, I meet many pastors. One Baptist pastor told me, "There are a lot of baptized pagans today. They are hell-doomed sinners, and they think because they have been baptized they are children of God." God says that an illegitimate son is not going to heaven—he shall not enter the congregation. God doesn't have illegitimate children. His children are all legitimate because they have been born again.

There is a good question for you to ask yourself today. Have you been born again? Do you know Christ as your Savior? "But as many as received him, to them gave he power to become the sons of God, even to them that believe on his name: which were born, not of blood, nor of the will of the flesh, nor of the will of man, but of God" (John 1:12–13). Do you qualify as a legitimate child of God? I don't care how many ceremonies you have been through, or how many churches you have joined, or how religious you may be—unless you are a child of the King, you are illegitimate.

FALSE RELIGIONS

An Ammonite or Moabite shall not enter into the congregation of the LORD; even to their tenth generation shall they not enter into the congregation of the LORD for ever:

Because they met you not with bread and with water in the way, when ye came forth out of Egypt; and because they hired against thee Balaam the son of Beor of Pethor of Mesopotamia, to curse thee [Deut. 23:3–4].

Archaeologists have discovered that the Ammonites and the Moabites were pagan to the worst degree. They have found a great many of their little images to Baal. False religion is not to enter into the congregation of the Lord. And how can one recognize false religion? "By their fruits ye shall know them." The evidence was that they "met you not with bread and water" in that great and terrible wilderness, and they hired Balaam to curse Israel.

Nevertheless the LORD thy God would not hearken unto Balaam; but the LORD thy God turned the curse into a blessing unto thee, because the LORD thy God loved thee.

Thou shalt not seek their peace nor their prosperity all thy days for ever [Deut. 23:5–6].

This sounds harsh, but it is a warning against linking up with false religions. False religion is satanic in origin. The Devil is not to enter into the congregation of the Lord. It is false religion that has damned this world more than anything else. It is possible for a beautiful church building with a high steeple and a lovely organ to be the very den of Satan. We are to beware of false religion. False religion has no place in the congregation of the Lord.

Thou shalt not abhor an Edomite; for he is thy brother: thou shalt not abhor an Egyptian; because thou wast a stranger in his land [Deut. 23:7].

We saw back in the Book of Genesis that Edom is Esau, and Esau and Jacob were twin brothers. Ammon and Moab were to be abhored. Why not Edom also? Because an Edomite was their brother.

For the believer, Esau represents our old nature, the flesh. We can hate the flesh, try to step on it, try to punish it, or mutilate it, but none of that will do any good. We are not to abhor the flesh, but we are not to yield to it. The old nature is not to control us. The flesh is in rebellion against God, but it is a part of us, and hating it will not get us anywhere.

They were not to abhor an Egyptian. Why? "Because thou wast a stranger in his land."

Egypt in Scripture represents the world. We are told, "Love not the world, neither the things that are in the world. If any man love the world, the love of the Father is not in him" (1 John 2:15). Again let me say that this does not mean we are not to appreciate the beauties of nature or our homes, our cars, and other conveniences that are part of the world around us. The point is that we are not to fall in love with these things. Of course we are not to despise them, but we are not to love them. You and I are strangers and pilgrims down here in this world. Just as the children of Israel were never called upon to plant flowers in the wilderness, neither are we called upon to join movements that try to straighten out the world. We are to give out the Word of God—that is our business—but we are pilgrims and strangers here, just passing through.

CLEANLINESS

Now beginning with verse 9 is a section on cleanliness. Even when they were out in the field of battle, they were to maintain a clean camp.

Thou shalt have a place also without the camp, whither thou shalt go forth abroad:

And thou shalt have a paddle upon thy weapon; and it shall be, when thou wilt ease thyself abroad, thou shalt

dig therewith, and shalt turn back and cover that which cometh from thee [Deut. 23:12–13].

God is interested in sanitation. Wherever Christianity has gone, there has been an improvement in sanitary conditions.

We hear so much about pollution today. Who polluted this universe? Certainly, it was not God who did it. He gave us clean streams, clean air, clean water. It is sin, sinful man, who pollutes this earth today. If men would follow the rules which God has given, this earth would be a sanitary place.

For the Lord thy God walketh in the midst of thy camp, to deliver thee, and to give up thine enemies before thee; therefore shall thy camp be holy: that he see no unclean thing in thee, and turn away from thee [Deut. 23:14].

God is interested in cleanliness. I think it was Webster who said that cleanliness is next to godliness. I think it is even closer than that—I would classify cleanliness as a part of godliness. God wants us clean in body, clean in environment, clean in thought, clean in action. We are to be a holy people in this world today. Say, this book is very practical, is it not?

There shall be no whore of the daughters of Israel, nor a sodomite of the sons of Israel.

Thou shalt not bring the hire of a whore, or the price of a dog, into the house of the Lord thy God for any vow: for even both these are abomination unto the Lord thy God [Deut. 23:17–18].

God said there were not to be harlots or sodomites among His people. God says that under no circumstance will He accept income from that which is illegal or from that which is immoral or wrong. He does not want any of it.

Now I am going to say something that I know is not popular to say. I do not believe that any Christian organization should receive money from any industry that is illegal or immoral. I thank God for the two schools that turned down a gift from a large brewery. Many questionable businesses try to gain respectability by giving to charity, as you know.

> **Thou shalt not lend upon usury to thy brother; usury of money, usury of victuals, usury of any thing that is lent upon usury:**

> **Unto a stranger thou mayest lend upon usury: but unto thy brother thou shalt not lend upon usury: that the LORD thy God may bless thee in all that thou settest thine hand to in the land whither thou goest to possess it [Deut. 23:19–20].**

Here again God is insisting that they take care of their brother. And if they lend money, they are not to charge him usury, which is interest.

> **When thou shalt vow a vow unto the LORD thy God, thou shalt not slack to pay it: for the LORD thy God will surely require it of thee and it would be sin in thee.**

> **But if thou shalt forbear to vow, it shall be no sin in thee [Deut. 23:21–22].**

A vow to the Lord was a voluntary act. No one was required to take a vow. However, once a person had made a vow to the Lord, that vow was absolutely binding, as we have mentioned before.

> **When thou comest into thy neighbour's vineyard, then thou mayest eat grapes thy fill at thine own pleasure; but thou shalt not put any in thy vessel.**

> **When thou comest into the standing corn of thy neighbour, then thou mayest pluck the ears with thine hand;**

but thou shalt not move a sickle unto thy neighbour's standing corn [Deut. 23:24–25].

We will find that the disciples of our Lord did this very thing. Because they were hungry, they began to pluck the grain and eat it as they passed through a field. As we see here in Deuteronomy, this was not illegal. God said that a farmer was to extend this courtesy.

CHAPTER 24

THEME: Divorce

This chapter begins with the Mosaic Law of divorce. The remainder of the chapter is devoted to people-to-people relationships in which mercy is to be shown. Friends, God is merciful, and He expects His people to exhibit mercy toward each other.

THE MOSAIC LAW OF DIVORCE

When a man hath taken a wife, and married her, and it come to pass that she find no favor in his eyes, because he hath found some uncleanness in her: then let him write her a bill of divorcement, and give it in her hand, and send her out of his house.

And when she is departed out of his house, she may go and be another man's wife.

And if the latter husband hate her, and write her a bill of divorcement, and giveth it in her hand, and sendeth her out of his house; or if the latter husband die, which took her to be his wife;

Her former husband, which sent her away, may not take her again to be his wife, after that she is defiled; for that is abomination before the LORD: and thou shalt not cause the land to sin, which the LORD thy God giveth thee for an inheritance [Deut. 24:1–4].

Now you may wonder why remarriage was put on that kind of basis. Well, because God doesn't agree to wife-swapping, which this would amount to. There is to be no trading back and forth.

This seems like a very easy form of divorce, does it not? It was very

easy. Why did God permit it? Well, the Lord Jesus was approached
with that question. "They say unto him, Why did Moses then command to give a writing of divorcement, and to put her away? He saith
unto them, Moses because of the hardness of your hearts suffered you
to put away your wives: but from the beginning it was not so. And I
say unto you, Whosoever shall put away his wife, except it be for for-
nication, and shall marry another committeth adultery: and whoso
marrieth her which is put away doth commit adultery" (Matt. 19:7–
9). Unfaithfulness to the marriage vow was the only grounds for divorce. (There is some speculation about 1 Corinthians 7 opening up
another reason or basis for divorce.)

Jesus said that Moses was permitted to make this law because of
the hardness of their hearts. There are a great many things which God
permits in His permissive will. He permits it because of the hardness
of our hearts. This is still true today in many cases of divorce. It is also
true in many of our homes, and it is true in the personal lives of many
individuals. God is merciful and gracious to us and permits things in
our lives that are not in His direct will. It is His permissive will that
manifests His grace to us. Knowing this, it would behoove some of the
more spiritual brethren not to be so critical of other folk today.

**When a man hath taken a new wife, he shall not go out
to war, neither shall he be charged with any business:
but he shall be free at home one year, and shall cheer up
his wife which he hath taken [Deut. 24:5].**

God protects the home even in the time of war. God regards the sacred-
ness of the marriage vow.

VARIED REGULATIONS

**If a man be found stealing any of his brethren of the
children of Israel, and maketh merchandise of him, or
selleth him; then that thief shall die; and thou shalt put
evil away from among you [Deut. 24:7].**

God condemns slavery. There is no question about that.

> **When thou beatest thine olive tree, thou shalt not go over the boughs again: it shall be for the stranger, for the fatherless, and for the widow.**
>
> **When thou gatherest the grapes of thy vineyard, thou shalt not glean it afterward: it shall be for the stranger, for the fatherless, and for the widow.**
>
> **And thou shalt remember that thou wast a bondman in the land of Egypt: therefore I command thee to do this thing [Deut. 24:20–22].**

God was taking care of those who were helpless, those less fortunate ones. God had a good poverty program, and the interesting thing is that it worked. We will see this a little later on when we get to the Book of Ruth.

CHAPTER 25

THEME: Punishment of the guilty; law protecting widows; judgment of Amalek

This is a remarkable chapter that expresses God's concern for protecting the innocent by punishing the guilty and by perpetuating a brother's name in Israel. It concludes with the command to "blot out the remembrance of Amalek from under heaven."

FORTY STRIPES

There were certain crimes that arose through difficulties between individuals. I think that in our legal nomenclature today we would call them misdemeanors. These would not be serious crimes which would merit the death sentence. However, they would require punishment.

> If there be a controversy between men, and they come unto judgment, that the judges may judge them; then they shall justify the righteous, and condemn the wicked.
>
> And it shall be, if the wicked man be worthy to be beaten, that the judge shall cause him to lie down, and to be beaten before his face, according to his fault, by a certain number.
>
> Forty stripes he may give him, and not exceed: lest, if he should exceed, and beat him above these with many stripes, then thy brother should seem vile unto thee [Deut. 25:1–3].

Forty stripes would be the limit. Otherwise there would be the danger of killing the man. The number of the stripes, one to forty, depended on the seriousness of the crime.

This method of punishment has gone entirely out of style. It was interesting to me to hear several outstanding attorneys discussing this. They agreed that it would break up a great deal of this lawlessness if there were public floggings. That is, when a person commits a minor crime, instead of putting him in an air-conditioned jail to loaf for a few days, he should be taken out and publicly flogged. Apparently God thought that is the way it should be handled, and the answer as to whether or not it was effective is found in the fact that Israel had a very low crime level.

THE OX NOT TO BE MUZZLED

Thou shalt not muzzle the ox when he treadeth out the corn [Deut. 25:4].

Here is a lovely thing. God is protecting the ox. When I was in Israel, I took pictures of this very thing because they still do this over there. For a long time I watched an Arab who had his ox going round and round, treading out the corn, and, do you know, he had his ox muzzled. God had said, "Don't do that. The ox is working for you; he is treading out your corn—let him eat." God's concern is a very wonderful thing.

It is interesting that Paul reaches into the Book of Deuteronomy and uses this verse in his letter to the Corinthian Christians. "For it is written in the law of Moses, Thou shalt not muzzle the mouth of the ox that treadeth out the corn. Doth God take care for oxen? Or saith he it altogether for our sakes? For our sakes, no doubt, this is written: that he that ploweth should plow in hope; and that he that thresheth in hope should be partaker of his hope. If we have sown unto you spiritual things, is it a great thing if we shall reap your carnal things? (1 Cor. 9:9–11). Do you see how Paul is applying this? He is saying, "Pay your preacher." "Even so hath the Lord ordained that they which preach the gospel should live of the gospel" (1 Cor. 9:14). The man who is ministering to you in spiritual things is feeding you spiritual food. You, in turn, are to feed him with material things. That is how Paul is making the application of this verse.

While I sit and talk into a microphone, making a record on tape for broadcasting on radio, I see the tape going round and round, and I feel like an ox treading out the corn. And you know, that is what I am trying to do—tread out the corn. God says not to muzzle the ox that treads out the corn. I'll let you make your own application of that!

LAW PROTECTING WIDOWS

Now we move on to another point. You can't make me believe that God does not have a sense of humor. God has a law here to take care of widows. It worked effectively, as we shall see in the Book of Ruth. But to me it is very humorous.

> **If brethren dwell together, and one of them die, and have no child, the wife of the dead shall not marry without unto a stranger: her husband's brother shall go in unto her, and take her to him to wife, and perform the duty of an husband's brother unto her.**

> **And it shall be, that the firstborn which she beareth shall succeed in the name of his brother which is dead, that his name be not put out of Israel [Deut. 25:5–6].**

God was protecting womanhood. We hear a great deal about women's rights, and it is interesting that God guarded their rights. We need to remember that in Israel most of the people were farmers. The land was divided among the people and each had his own piece of land. When a man died, he could leave a farm with all his wheat and corn and also his livestock of sheep and oxen. The widow was left with this farm to care for. Suppose some man from the outside, a foreigner, or a man from another tribe wanted to marry her and thus come into possession of the land. This was forbidden. She was not permitted to marry outside. Here is a case where the widow does the proposing. What she was to do was to go and claim one of her husband's brothers, a cousin, or the nearest relative and ask him to marry her.

And if the man like not to take his brother's wife, then
let his brother's wife go up to the gate unto the elders,
and say, My husband's brother refuseth to raise up unto
his brother a name in Israel, he will not perform the
duty of my husband's brother [Deut. 25:7].

If the brother, or relative, doesn't want to marry her, she can take him
to court, you see.

Then the elders of his city shall call him, and speak
unto him: and if he stand to it, and say, I like not to take
her;

Then shall his brother's wife come unto him in the presence of the elders, and loose his shoe from off his foot,
and spit in his face, and shall answer and say, So shall it
be done unto that man that will not build up his brother's house.

And his name shall be called in Israel, The house of him
that hath his shoe loosed [Deut. 25:8–10].

If the man refused to marry her, the woman could take him to court—
the city gate was where court was held in those days. She would tell
the elders how it was. If he still refuses to marry the widow, there is a
penalty. He is disgraced for not performing that which he should do
according to the law. It reveals the fact that he is not being true to his
brother, or to his family, or to his tribe, or to his nation, or to his God.
The man is disgraced.

Here is a marvelous example of how God protected the widow. We
will see this law in operation when we get to the Book of Ruth. It was
used effectively in that book.

Can you imagine how this would affect a family in Israel? Suppose
there was a family of four sons living on a farm in Ephraim country.
Suppose that night after night one of the boys went off with the lan-
tern and when he came back to go to bed, he would be whistling.

Pretty soon the family would get into a huddle and the brothers would ask him, "Where are you going every evening?" They'd do a little investigating of their own and find there was a daughter in the family that lived down the road. So the brother would admit, "I believe in the good-neighbor policy, and I have been going down there to visit that family that just moved in." And he would admit that he was thinking of marrying the girl. Now, if those brothers didn't care too much for that girl, can you imagine what would happen? They'd say, "Listen—before you get any notions, you go the doctor and have a physical check-up. We want to be sure you are in good health before you marry her, because none of us want to get stuck with her." Believe me, they got down to business. Getting married was a family affair. This was God's way of drawing families very close together, of protecting the widows, and also of protecting the land. You see, this was the way the land would always stay in the same family. It was a very good law for them.

The next verses give a severe punishment for involvement when men strive together. Also God commands His people to be accurate in their measurements and in their weights. They are to be absolutely honest in their business dealings.

JUDGMENT OF AMALEK

In Exodus 17 we have the record of Amalek's attack upon the children of Israel when they came out of Egypt. The Amalekites were marauding nomads out on that desert.

Remember what Amalek did unto thee by the way, when ye were come forth out of Egypt;

How he met thee by the way, and smote the hindmost of thee, even all that were feeble behind thee, when thou wast faint and weary; and he feared not God.

Therefore it shall be, when the LORD thy God hath given thee rest from all thine enemies round about, in the land which the LORD thy God giveth thee for an inheritance to

possess it, that thou shalt blot out the remembrance of Amalek from under heaven; thou shalt not forget it [Deut. 25:17–19].

Israel had suffered an unprovoked attack by Amalek at Rephidim. That was the battle when Moses was on the top of the mountain and Aaron and Hur held up his arms in prayer to God. When his hands were up, Joshua and the army of Israel won; when his hands were down, they lost. They finally won a victory over Amalek. At that time the Lord said a very interesting thing, ". . . thou shalt blot out the remembrance of Amalek from under heaven."

As I have mentioned before, Amalek represents the flesh; that is, the fallen nature we inherited from Adam. God intends eventually to get rid of that old nature—it would be impossible to go to heaven with it. You and I have an old nature that can never be obedient unto God. We will deal with this subject quite thoroughly when we get to the Epistle to the Romans. Amalek is an illustration of the flesh. As long as we are in this life, we shall never get rid of the flesh—"Because the LORD hath sworn that the LORD will have war with Amalek from generation to generation" (Exod. 17:16). We saw in chapter 23 that the flesh is not for us to despise. We cannot overcome the flesh by becoming ascetic or by trying to beat it down or by becoming super-pious. That won't accomplish anything. But we do need to recognize that there is a war going on in each one of us. It is a war between the spirit and the flesh.

"For the flesh lusteth against the Spirit, and the Spirit against the flesh: and these are contrary the one to the other: so that ye cannot do the things that ye would" (Gal. 5:17). We cannot overcome the flesh by fighting. The only way we can overcome the flesh is by yielding to the Spirit of God. Only the Spirit of God can produce the fruits of the Spirit in our lives. The Lord says that He is going to blot out the remembrances of Amalek from under heaven. I thank God that He intends to get rid of the flesh someday!

CHAPTER 26

The chapter before us presents the beautiful ceremony in connection with the offering of firstfruits. Acknowledging that all the produce of the land came from God, and as an expression of thankfulness for His goodness, the Israelites brought as an offering to Him a portion of the fruit that ripened first.

> And it shall be, when thou art come in unto the land which the LORD thy God giveth thee for an inheritance, and possessest it, and dwellest therein;
>
> That thou shalt take of the first of all the fruit of the earth, which thou shalt bring of thy land that the LORD thy God giveth thee, and shalt put it in a basket, and shalt go unto the place which the LORD thy God shall choose to place his name there.
>
> And thou shalt go unto the priest that shall be in those days, and say unto him, I profess this day unto the LORD thy God, that I am come unto the country which the LORD sware unto our fathers for to give us.
>
> And the priest shall take the basket out of thine hand, and set it down before the altar of the LORD thy God [Deut. 26:1–4].

As he presented his offering of firstfruits to the Lord, he was to review God's gracious dealings with his people in delivering them from oppression in Egypt and in bringing them to the bountiful land He had promised them.

> And thou shalt speak and say before the LORD thy God, A Syrian ready to perish was my father, and he went

> down into Egypt, and sojourned there with a few, and
> became there a nation, great, mighty, and populous
> [Deut. 26:5].

There is something here I would like to have you note. He comes to God first with confession. The Israelite would confess, "A Syrian ready to perish was my father." Was Abraham an Israelite? No, he actually was not. What about Isaac? Well, he was not either. What about Jacob? Technically, Jacob was not an Israelite. The crowd that went down to Egypt were Syrians. Abraham was no more an Israelite than he was an Ishmaelite—since both peoples descended from him. Abraham was a Syrian as to nationality.

> And the Egyptians evil entreated us, and afflicted us,
> and laid upon us hard bondage:
>
> And when we cried unto the LORD God of our fathers, the
> LORD heard our voice, and looked on our affliction, and
> our labour, and our oppression:
>
> And the LORD brought us forth out of Egypt with a
> mighty hand, and with an outstretched arm, and with
> great terribleness, and with signs, and with wonders:
>
> And he hath brought us into this place, and hath given
> us this land, even a land that floweth with milk and
> honey.
>
> And now, behold, I have brought the firstfruits of the
> land, which thou, O LORD, hast given me. And thou
> shalt set it before the Lord thy God, and worship before
> the LORD thy God [Deut. 26:6–10].

To the Israelite it was to be a time of true thanksgiving. Thanksgiving for us is a day when we bring a sacrifice of praise and thanksgiving unto God—and that's good. Most of us, and I confess I am in the category, eat a big turkey dinner. Usually friends invite us out to dinner. This past Thanksgiving was a glorious time. But how many of us really make an offering to God on Thanksgiving Day? Israel did—this was the beginning of Thanksgiving. If we go back and check the Pilgrims and the Puritans, we will find that they, out of their meager resources, made an offering unto God on that day. Wonderful as it is to make an offering of thanksgiving and praise with our lips, we ought to back it up with our purse. Praise and purse go together in God's Word.

The second part of this chapter deals with the Israelites' declaration of obedience to God.

When thou hast made an end of tithing all the tithes of thine increase the third year, which is the year of tithing, and hast given it unto the Levite, the stranger, the fatherless, and the widow, that they may eat within thy gates, and be filled;

Then thou shalt say before the Lord thy God, I have brought away the hallowed things out of mine house, and also have given them unto the Levite, and unto the stranger, to the fatherless, and to the widow, according to all thy commandments which thou hast commanded me: I have not transgressed thy commandments, neither have I forgotten them [Deut. 26:12–13].

If Israel would keep His commandments, He promises to make them His peculiar people and to place them above all nations of the earth.

CHAPTER 27

THEME: The future of the land: curses for disobedience

We come now to one of the most vital sections of the Book of Deuteronomy. This is now Moses' third oration. It belongs to the next major section of the book which is regarding the future in the land. This is the third main section of the book and extends from chapter 27—30. In it we find the so-called Palestinian covenant which God made with the nation Israel.

I have called Deuteronomy 28—30 the pre-written history of Israel in the land before they enter the land. The section from Deuteronomy 29—30:10 is the Palestinian covenant.

As we begin this new section, I think we ought to say something about a covenant. That word has occurred several times already. There are different kinds of covenants. We find that individuals make covenants with each other. There are covenants of this kind mentioned in the Bible. Then there are nations that make covenants, and some of them are mentioned in the Bible. Then there are the covenants which God made with His people and with all humanity in the Old Testament. We have already studied the Adamic covenant, the Noahic covenant, the Abrahamic covenant, and the Mosaic covenant. Now we have come to the Palestinian covenant.

The covenants which God makes are divided into two different classifications: conditional and unconditional. We could call them eternal covenants and temporary covenants. The eternal covenant is a permanent covenant and it is unconditional. The temporary covenant is a conditional covenant. It is important to distinguish between the two.

The covenant which God made with Abraham was an unconditional covenant. The covenant God made with Moses, the Ten Commandments, was a conditional covenant—"Now therefore, *if* ye will obey my voice indeed, and keep my covenant, then . . ." (Exod. 19:5).

The Palestinian covenant which God made in the chapters we are about to study is an unconditional covenant.

This covenant has to do with Israel's future. We understand that these people are now standing on the east bank of the Jordan River. They are preparing to enter the land. This is the new generation; the old generation has died in the wilderness. Moses himself will not enter into the land. We shall see that this book closes with a requiem to Moses. He dies, but the people enter the land under a new leader. Now this particular section is prophetic and has to do with their future in the land which they are about to enter. We find here some of the most remarkable prophecies in the entire Word of God.

And Moses with the elders of Israel commanded the people, saying, Keep all the commandments which I command you this day.

And it shall be on the day when ye shall pass over Jordan unto the land which the LORD thy God giveth thee, that thou shalt set thee up great stones, and plaster them with plaster:

And thou shalt write upon them all the words of this law, when thou art passed over, that thou mayest go in unto the land which the LORD thy God giveth thee, a land that floweth with milk and honey; as the LORD God of thy fathers hath promised thee [Deut. 27:1-3].

They were told that when they crossed over into the land, the Ten Commandments were to be written in stone and displayed. Their tenure in the land, their dwelling there, would be determined by their obedience to God. That was a conditional arrangement. But the *land* was given to them with no conditions attached whatsoever. God has given that land to Israel, and that is an unconditional covenant. God will bring Israel back into that land because it belongs to them. That is something very important for us to realize at the present time.

Therefore it shall be when ye be gone over Jordan, that ye shall set up these stones, which I command you this day, in mount Ebal, and thou shalt plaster them with plaster.

And there shalt thou build an altar unto the LORD thy God, an altar of stones: thou shalt not lift up any iron tool upon them.

Thou shalt build the altar of the LORD thy God of whole stones: and thou shalt offer burnt offerings thereon unto the LORD thy God:

And thou shalt offer peace offerings, and shalt eat there, and rejoice before the LORD thy God.

And thou shalt write upon the stones all the words of this law very plainly [Deut. 27:4–8].

God's Law was to be prominently displayed. In fact, it was to be put in front of them wherever they went—even on the doorposts of their homes.

And Moses and the priests the Levites spake unto all Israel, saying, Take heed, and hearken, O Israel; this day thou art become the people of the LORD thy God.

Thou shalt therefore obey the voice of the LORD thy God, and do his commandments and his statutes, which I command thee this day.

And Moses charged the people the same day, saying,

These shall stand upon mount Gerizim to bless the people, when ye are come over Jordan; Simeon, and Levi, and Judah, and Issachar, and Joseph, and Benjamin [Deut. 27:9–12].

When they get into the Promised Land, the blessing of the people is to be declared from Mount Gerizim. He mentions the tribes who will do the blessing.

> **And these shall stand upon mount Ebal to curse; Reuben, Gad, and Asher, and Zebulun, Dan, and Naphtali [Deut. 27:13].**

The tribes who are to declare the curses are to go over to Mount Ebal. These mountains are in the area where the Samaritan woman was at the well. That well is still there today. The blessings were from Mount Gerizim and the curses from Mount Ebal.

Now a list of the curses is given. After they are in the land, their tenure there is on a condition. We might say that each generation is a tenant and it is to pay rent. God is the land owner, and that rent is *obedience* to God. Actually, the nation is more than a tenant because God has given Israel that land as an eternal possession. However, when a generation would not obey God, that generation would be put out of the land, even though the land remained theirs as an eternal inheritance. This is the reason that that piece of real estate is the most sensitive spot on the topside of this globe. It is the belief of a great many people that right now a world war could be triggered by what takes place in that land, and certainly this is true.

There are twelve curses given here, and I am not going into detail about them as they are self-explanatory.

> **Cursed be the man that maketh any graven or molten image, an abomination unto the LORD, the work of the hands of the craftsman, and putteth it in a secret place. And all the people shall answer and say, Amen [Deut. 27:15].**

This has to do with the first two of the Ten Commandments.

> **Cursed be he that setteth light by his father or his mother. And all the people shall say, Amen [Deut. 27:16].**

This deals with the fifth of the Ten Commandments.

**Cursed be he that confirmeth not all the words of this
law to do them. And all the people shall say, Amen
[Deut. 27:26].**

As you read all the verses in this chapter, you will see that they all deal
with the breaking of the Ten Commandments.

CHAPTER 28

THEME: Israel's pre-written history

This chapter continues the section regarding the future of Israel. Moses pronounces the conditional part of the covenant. The people of Israel would be blessed only as they obeyed God. Their disobedience would bring curses, which are spelled out for them here.

Then we have one of the most remarkable passages of Scripture which gives their pre-written history in the land before they had even set foot on it. There are three prophecies of their dispossession—all have been fulfilled. There are three prophecies of their restoration—two have been fulfilled. Israel's third return to the land is yet future.

> **And it shall come to pass, if thou shalt hearken diligently unto the voice of the LORD thy God, to observe and to do all his commandments which I command thee this day, that the LORD thy God will set thee on high above all nations of the earth:**
>
> **And all these blessings shall come on thee, and overtake thee, if thou shalt hearken unto the voice of the LORD thy God [Deut. 28:1–2].**

"*If* thou shalt hearken diligently"—notice the great big "if." This is a conditional part of the covenant. They are going to be blessed only as they obey God.

> **Blessed shalt thou be in the city, and blessed shalt thou be in the field.**
>
> **Blessed shall be the fruit of thy body, and the fruit of thy ground, and the fruit of thy cattle, the increase of thy kine, and the flocks of thy sheep.**
>
> **Blessed shall be thy basket and thy store.**

Blessed shalt thou be when thou comest in, and blessed shalt thou be when thou goest out [Deut. 28:3–6].

As you read this, perhaps you are struck by the fact that there are twelve curses pronounced but there are only six blessings. If you want to know why this is so, I'll tell you where we pick up the rest of the blessings. Our Lord stood on the mount and delivered what is called the Sermon on the Mount. How did He begin it? *"Blessed* are the poor in spirit: for theirs is the kingdom of heaven" (Matt. 5:3)—then the other beatitudes follow. Beginning His message like this would make the instructed Israelite listen. He was hearing of the blessings which would come to them even after their long, checkered history. At that time they had already experienced captivity twice, and they were yet to go into another captivity that would scatter them throughout the entire earth.

There is the promise of an abundance of blessing if they will obey.

And the LORD shall make thee the head, and not the tail; and thou shalt be above only, and thou shalt not be beneath; if that thou hearken unto the commandments of the LORD thy God, which I command thee this day, to observe and to do them:

And thou shalt not go aside from any of the words which I command thee this day, to the right hand, or to the left, to go after other gods to serve them [Deut. 28:13–14].

Now he returns to the curses and mentions that they all rest upon this matter of an "if."

But it shall come to pass, if thou wilt not hearken unto the voice of the LORD thy God, to observe to do all his commandments and his statutes which I command thee this day; that all these curses shall come upon thee, and overtake thee [Deut. 28:15].

Again we see that this is conditional.

Now we come to one of the most remarkable passages of Scripture. It is the history of Israel in the land, pre-written. Scripture prophesied concerning Israel's being dispossessed out of the land three times and regathered into the land three times. There are to be three dispossessions and three regatherings of Israel.

The first of these was prophesied by God to Abraham. "Know of a surety that thy seed shall be a stranger in a land that is not theirs and shall serve them; and they shall afflict them four hundred years. . . . But in the fourth generation they shall come hither again . . . (Gen. 15:13, 16). They went down into Egypt for 430 years; then God brought them out of Egypt. That is what we are following now in Deuteronomy. They are on the east bank of the Jordan River, and God is bringing them back to the land for the first regathering. In the Book of Joshua, we will find them entering into the land, and in the Book of Judges we will find them settled in the land, which is a complete and literal fulfillment.

Now, before they have even entered the land, the second time they are to be put out of the land is mentioned here. This is a very remarkable chapter.

Thy sons and thy daughters shall be given unto another people, and thine eyes shall look, and fail with longing for them all the day long: and there shall be no might in thine hand.

The fruit of thy land, and all thy labours, shall a nation which thou knowest not eat up; and thou shalt be only oppressed and crushed alway:

So that thou shalt be mad for the sight of thine eyes which thou shalt see [Deut. 28:32–34].

This verse was accurately fulfilled in Judah's last king, Zedekiah, whose sons were slain before him; then his eyes were put out. Blind and helpless, he was carried away into Babylonian captivity.

The LORD shall smite thee in the knees, and in the legs, with a sore botch that cannot be healed, from the sole of thy foot unto the top of thy head.

The LORD shall bring thee, and thy king which thou shalt set over thee, unto a nation which neither thou nor thy fathers have known; and there shalt thou serve other gods, wood and stone.

And thou shalt become an astonishment, a proverb, and a byword, among all nations whither the LORD shall lead thee [Deut. 28:35–37].

This was to be the Babylonian captivity which is now a matter of history. We have the record. We will learn of it later in our study of the Bible where we will read more prohecies about it and then will actually see it come to pass in both Kings and Chronicles.

Why did all this happen to them? It was because of their disobedience. God had given them the "if's." God said, "If you obey, you will be blessed. If you disobey, you will be put out of the land."

Israel was regathered from the Babylonian captivity. Their return to the land is recorded in Ezra and Nehemiah. The prophets Haggai, Zechariah, and Malachi tell of their return to the land. So then, this is the second prophecy concerning their return to the land. This has been literally fulfilled.

The third scattering of Israel was the result of being conquered by Rome. This is described prophetically.

Therefore shalt thou serve thine enemies which the LORD shall send against thee, in hunger, and in thirst, and in nakedness, and in want of all things: and he shall put a yoke of iron upon thy neck, until he have destroyed thee [Deut. 28:48].

Here in my study I have two volumes of Flavius Josephus' history in which he tells about the coming of the Romans under Titus. Rome, known as the iron kingdom, fulfilled the prediction. "He shall put a yoke of iron upon thy neck."

The LORD shall bring a nation against thee from far, from the end of the earth, as swift as the eagle flieth; a nation whose tongue thou shalt not understand [Deut. 28:49].

Rome, coming all the way from the West, spoke a language that was entirely different from Hebrew. Our English is based on Latin and the European languages, but Hebrew is a language that is related to the Asian and African and Oriental languages. It is altogether different. God says the conquerors would be people "whose tongue thou shalt not understand."

It is interesting that Rome carried standards bearing the emblem of the eagle. I am of the opinion that many an instructed Israelite, when he looked over the battlements of the wall and saw the standards of Titus with an eagle on them, said, "This is *it!*"

A nation of fierce countenance, which shall not regard the person of the old, nor shew favour to the young:

And he shall eat the fruit of thy cattle, and the fruit of thy land, until thou be destroyed: which also shall not leave thee either corn, wine, or oil, or the increase of thy kine, or flocks of thy sheep, until he have destroyed thee.

And he shall besiege thee in all thy gates, until thy high and fenced walls come down, wherein thou trustedst, throughout all thy land: and he shall besiege thee in all thy gates throughout all thy land, which the LORD thy God hath given thee.

And thou shalt eat the fruit of thine own body, the flesh of thy sons and of thy daughters, which the LORD thy

God hath given thee, in the siege, and in the straitness,
wherewith thine enemies shall distress thee [Deut.
28:50–53].

Josephus tells in his history how mothers were forced to give up their
babies, and the flesh of the babies was eaten. The people died, and
their corpses collected inside the city. They had to throw them over
the wall. May I say to you that this prophecy was literally fulfilled.
And now the Jewish people are scattered throughout the world.

And the Lord shall scatter thee among all people, from
the one end of the earth even unto the other; and there
thou shalt serve other gods, which neither thou nor thy
fathers have known, even wood and stone [Deut. 28:64].

They have never returned from that dispersion. That has yet to be fulfilled. There are three prophecies of dispossessions. There are three
prophecies that they will return. They have returned twice. They have
not returned the third time.

So we have six prophecies. Five of them have been literally fulfilled. What do you think about the sixth one? I can tell you what I
think about it. I think it will be literally fulfilled. It is yet to come in
the future.

And among these nations shalt thou find no ease, neither shall the sole of thy foot have rest: but the Lord shall
give thee there a trembling heart, and failing of eyes,
and sorrow of mind:

And thy life shall hang in doubt before thee; and thou
shalt fear day and night, and shalt have none assurance
of thy life:

In the morning thou shalt say, Would God it were even!
and at even thou shalt say, Would God it were morning!
for the fear of thine heart wherewith thou shalt fear, and

for the sight of thine eyes which thou shalt see [Deut. 28:65–67].

How literally all this has been fulfilled in the persecutions of the Jews down through the centuries! This is all the consequence of their continued disobedience. They have no rest, and they have a trembling heart. In the morning they wish for evening, and in the evening they wish for morning. How sad. God is true to His Word, friends. What a lesson there is in that for us.

This should move us to tell the gospel to these people who are dispossessed from the land. The gospel of the Lord Jesus Christ is for Jew and Gentile alike, and it is for the "obedience to the faith among all nations" (Rom. 1:5).

CHAPTER 29

THEME: *Palestinian covenant (introduction)*

Chapters 29 and 30 are considered the Palestinian covenant. Dr. Lewis Sperry Chafer considers chapters 28—30 to be the covenant. *The Scofield Reference Bible* considers it to be 29—30:10 with chapter 29 as the introduction. In my notes I take chapter 29 through the first ten verses of chapter 30 as being the covenant, although the covenant proper is in the first ten verses of chapter 30. This chapter 29 is a preliminary.

RESUMÉ OF GOD'S CARE

This is now the fourth oration of Moses.

> **These are the words of the covenant, which the LORD commanded Moses to make with the children of Israel in the land of Moab, beside the covenant which he made with them in Horeb [Deut. 29:1].**

The covenant made in Horeb was the Ten Commandments or what we know as the Mosaic Law. The covenant which God is going to make with them here relates to the land, and it is called the Palestinian covenant. God makes this covenant with them just before they enter the land.

> **And Moses called unto all Israel, and said unto them, Ye have seen all that the LORD did before your eyes in the land of Egypt unto Pharaoh, and unto all his servants, and unto all his land [Deut. 29:2].**

These people would have been children and teenagers when they witnessed these things. The oldest people in the nation would have been about sixty years old after wandering through the wilderness since the failure at Kadesh-barnea. Only Joshua and Caleb remained of the old generation.

> **The great temptations which thine eyes have seen, the signs, and those great miracles:**
>
> **Yet the Lord hath not given you an heart to perceive, and eyes to see, and ears to hear, unto this day [Deut. 29:3-4].**

In spite of seeing all the signs, they still did not perceive. Isaiah has a great deal to say about that. Paul in Romans deals with the blindness of Israel. "(According as it is written, God hath given them the spirit of slumber, eyes that they should not see, and ears that they should not hear;) unto this day" (Rom. 11:8). Does this mean that God will not permit them to comprehend, that God turns them off? No, it means they are already off. God has to turn us on! That is something which we need to recognize today. Until God opens the eyes and the ears of men and women, they cannot hear the gospel. Now do not misunderstand me—they can hear the words, but they cannot hear the gospel with understanding.

A writer of a magazine article classified our program of going through the Bible in five years with religious racketeers. He seems to think that if you attempt to teach the Bible you are running a religious racket! I wish the man would listen to the program to see what we are trying to do. And yet I still feel frustrated because if he did listen, he wouldn't understand. He wouldn't be able to comprehend. He would still feel that we are teaching the Bible on the radio for some ulterior motive. He would feel that the Bible is just being used as propaganda. Why? Because it would take the Spirit of God to work through the Word of God to open his eyes and his heart. Then he would see that the Word of God is effective in the lives of many people.

Now God says that he just left these people as they were. They had no intention of turning to Him. They had broken communication with the living and true God. Therefore, God would just leave them in their state of unbelief.

And I have led you forty years in the wilderness: your clothes are not waxen old upon you, and thy shoe is not waxen old upon thy foot [Deut. 29:5].

Imagine walking for forty years in the same pair of shoes, and their not getting old! Now Moses goes on to describe their journey through the wilderness and how this should have opened their eyes.

A great many people today say that if God would only perform a miracle before their eyes, they would believe. Well, these children of Israel saw miracles for forty years, and yet they did not believe. It is not for want of evidence that men are unbelievers. They are unbelievers not because of what they read in the Bible nor because of what they see around them. The problem is on the inside. They are unbelievers because they are innately enemies of God. They have no capacity for the things of God. What a picture God presents of the human heart! He says that it is desperately wicked and that none of us can actually conceive how terrible it really is. "Because the carnal mind is enmity against God: for it is not subject to the law of God, neither indeed can be. So then they that are in the flesh cannot please God" (Rom. 8:7–8). Paul wrote this after God had tested Israel for about 1500 years under the Law. What a picture of humanity this is! Those who are in the flesh cannot please God.

Moses gives them a resumé of their history, reminding them of God's wonderful provision and care for them. This is the preliminary to the covenant.

Remember that the Palestinian covenant is unconditional, but that their tenure in the land will depend on their obedience.

Ye stand this day all of you before the LORD your God; your captains of your tribes, your elders, and your officers, with all the men of Israel,

Your little ones, your wives, and thy stranger that is in
thy camp, from the hewer of thy wood unto the drawer of
thy water:

That thou shouldest enter into covenant with the Lord
thy God, and into his oath, which the Lord thy God
maketh with thee this day:

That he may establish thee to-day for a people unto himself, and that he may be unto thee a God, as he hath said
unto thee, and as he hath sworn unto thy fathers, to
Abraham, to Isaac, and to Jacob [Deut. 29:10–13].

As we read Moses' warning that disobedience to the covenant will
affect both the people and the land, it sounds to us like a prediction,
because Israel did forsake the covenant.

So that the generation to come of your children that shall
rise up after you, and the stranger that shall come from
a far land, shall say, when they see the plagues of that
land, and the sicknesses which the Lord hath laid upon
it;

And that the whole land thereof is brimstone, and salt,
and burning, that it is not sown, nor beareth, nor any
grass groweth therein, like the overthrow of Sodom, and
Gomorrah, Admah, and Zeboim, which the Lord over-
threw in his anger, and in his wrath:

Even all nations shall say, Wherefore hath the Lord done
thus unto this land? what meaneth the heat of this great
anger?

Then men shall say, Because they have forsaken the covenant of the Lord God of their fathers, which he made
with them when he brought them forth out of the land of
Egypt:

For they went and served other gods, and worshipped them, gods whom they knew not, and whom he had not given unto them:

And the anger of the LORD was kindled against this land, to bring upon it all the curses that are written in this book [Deut. 29:22–27].

Years ago I heard the late Dr. George Gill tell about a trip he made by train, going down through Asia Minor and into Palestine. Late in the afternoon they were leaving Jerusalem and dropping down into the Dead Sea area. As they did, he was standing out on the back vestibule of the train with a very wealthy American. The American said, "I always heard this was the land of milk and honey. Why, I've never seen a land that is as bad as this. I've never seen anything like it." Dr. Gill said, "It is interesting that you said that." Then he opened his Bible and showed the American in verse 24 that strangers shall come from a far land and ask that very question, "Wherefore hath the LORD done thus unto this land? what meaneth the heat of this great anger?" and Dr. Gill told him the exact reason which Moses had given 3500 years ago. "Because they have forsaken the covenant the LORD God of their fathers."

The land and the people go together. Actually, the whole Mosaic system is geared for that land. It is not only for the people but also for that land. That is important to see. In our Lord's day, the Mount of Olives was covered with trees. It was a real wooded area. The enemies who came to conquer cut out all the timber and left the land desolate. God's judgment does not fall only on the people. It also has fallen on the land.

And the LORD rooted them out of their land in anger, and in wrath, and in great indignation, and cast them into another land, as it is this day.

The secret things belong unto the LORD our God: but those things which are revealed belong unto us and to

**our children for ever, that we may do all the words of
this law [Deut. 29:28–29].**

But even before the covenant is given, they are told what will ultimately happen.

Now friend, God hasn't told us a lot of things, but there are certain
things He has told us, and He surely has told us about that land. It lies
over there right now, desolate, and they are trying to get water on it.
Agricultural authorities have said that if the land could be revived by
getting water to it, it should be able to support fifteen to twenty-five
million people.

I have traveled in that land from Jericho to Jerusalem, back and
forth several times. Anyone who travels there is bound to ask, "What
meaneth all the judgment on the land of milk and honey?" Israel was
put out of the land because God said, "You go into it and live in it on
condition." They did not meet His condition; they did not obey Him.

Does this mean that since Israel failed to keep the covenant, they
will not go back to the land? No, God made the Palestinian covenant
with these people *unconditionally*. We shall see that in the next chapter.

CHAPTER 30

THEME: The Palestinian covenant

We come now to the Palestinian covenant which God made with Israel. Read it carefully. You will notice there are no "if's" in this covenant. It is an unconditional promise of future blessing.

> **And it shall come to pass, when all these things are come upon thee, the blessing and the curse, which I have set before thee, and thou shalt call them to mind among all the nations, whither the Lord thy God hath driven thee,**
>
> **And shalt return unto the Lord thy God, and shalt obey his voice according to all that I command thee this day, thou and thy children, with all thine heart, and with all thy soul [Deut. 30:1-2].**

There are seven great promises which God makes here. He makes these statements which are unconditional. Verse 1 tells that they will be dispersed among all the nations. The nation would be plucked off the land for its unfaithfulness. That has taken place.

Verse 2 tells that there will be a future repentance of Israel in the dispersion. They are going to come back to God. Someone may ask whether their return will be on the basis of their obedience. It seems logical that if they were dispersed because of disobedience, they will return because of their obedience. No, friend, this is the order of grace, not law. They will not be returned because of their obedience, but they will be obedient because of their return. God will bring them back to the land. The regathering of Israel into her own land is the theme of at least twelve major prophecies in the Old Testament. We will call your attention to them when we come to them.

> That then the Lᴏʀᴅ thy God will turn thy captivity, and
> have compassion upon thee, and will return and gather
> thee from all the nations, whither the Lᴏʀᴅ thy God hath
> scattered thee [Deut. 30:3].

This verse tells that their Messiah will return. Notice that, for it is very important. This is the first mention of the return of Christ to the earth that is recorded in Scripture. (When we get to the Book of Jude, we will find that Enoch mentioned the fact that He is coming back, but that was not recorded in the Old Testament.) This is a remarkable prophecy, and it has not yet been fulfilled. Not until its fulfillment will the land be blessed and be at peace.

> If any of thine be driven out unto the outmost parts of
> heaven, from thence with the Lᴏʀᴅ thy God gather thee,
> and from thence will he fetch thee:
>
> And the Lᴏʀᴅ thy God will bring thee into the land
> which thy fathers possessed, and thou shalt possess it;
> and he will do thee good, and multiply thee above thy
> fathers [Deut. 30:4–5].

Here is the fourth great promise of God. Israel is to be restored to the land. This is an unconditional promise. No amount of scattering can change the fact that in the future God will bring them into the land, as verse 4 makes clear.

The fifth promise is that there will be a national conversion.

> And the Lᴏʀᴅ thy God will circumcise thine heart, and
> the heart of thy seed, to love the Lᴏʀᴅ thy God with all
> thine heart, and with all thy soul, that thou mayest live
> [Deut. 30:6].

We find this same promise reaffirmed in Jeremiah and Hosea and stated by Paul in the Book of Romans.

The sixth thing mentioned here is that Israel's enemies will be judged. Israel will return and then obey the voice of the Lord. That is the order of grace. And then their enemies will be judged.

> And the LORD thy God will put all these curses upon thine enemies, and on them that hate thee, which persecuted thee.

> And thou shalt return and obey the voice of the LORD, and do all his commandments which I command thee this day [Deut. 30:7–8].

Finally, the seventh wonderful thing is that Israel will then receive her full blessing.

> And the LORD thy God will make thee plenteous in every work of thine hand, in the fruit of thy body, and in the fruit of thy cattle, and in the fruit of thy land, for good: for the LORD will again rejoice over thee for good, as he rejoiced over thy fathers:

> If thou shalt hearken unto the voice of the LORD thy God, to keep his commandments and his statutes which are written in this book of the law, and if thou turn unto the LORD thy God with all thine heart, and with all thy soul [Deut. 30:9–10].

When will the day of return be? Is it actually happening now? We cannot be dogmatic about what we do not know. It clearly states that when they return to the land, it will be in obedience to God. There will be no blessing for them in the land until the time when they return in obedience with the new heart which God will give them. This will be at the time when God returns them to the land. The present return to Israel is not in obedience to God. I believe that the return of Israel under the covenant promise is yet in the future. It is unconditional because it is God who will return them to the land.

For this commandment which I command thee this day, it is not hidden from thee, neither is it far off.

It is not in heaven, that thou shouldest say, Who shall go up for us to heaven, and bring it unto us, that we may hear it, and do it?

Neither is it beyond the sea, that thou shouldest say, Who shall go over the sea for us, and bring it unto us, that we may hear it, and do it?

But the word is very nigh unto thee, in thy mouth, and in thy heart, that thou mayest do it [Deut. 30:11–14].

Israel can plead no excuse that they do not know the commandment of God. God has brought it right to them, and they know it.

We also have a responsibility—we who live in the land where we can hear the gospel. My friend, you don't have to go to heaven to get salvation. You don't need to cross the ocean to get it. May I say to you, it's right near you. It is as near as your radio; it is as near to you as a preacher or another Christian who will give you the Word of God. And you are responsible to act upon what you have heard. That is where your free will comes in. It is my business to get out the Word of God—I try to get it right up to your eardrums by radio, and right before your eyes by the printed page. That is as far as I can go. From then on, it is up to you.

Now notice that verses 12 and 13 are quoted by the apostle Paul in Romans. "But the righteousness which is of faith speaketh on this wise, Say not in thine heart, Who shall ascend into heaven? (that is, to bring Christ down from above:) Or, Who shall descend into the deep? (that is, to bring up Christ again from the dead.) But what saith it? The word is nigh thee, even in thy mouth, and in thy heart: that is, the word of faith, which we preach; that if thou shalt confess with thy mouth the Lord Jesus, and shalt believe in thine heart that God hath raised him from the dead, thou shalt be saved. For with the heart man believeth unto righteousness; and with the mouth confession is made unto salvation" (Rom. 10:6–10).

Paul does not say that Moses said this, but rather the "of-faith-righteousness" is the speaker. Paul is not making a substitution of faith here for the Law. The passage in Deuteronomy is prophetic and speaks of a day when Israel will turn to God with all their heart and soul. (See Deut. 33:10.) It looks forward to the new covenant which God will make with Israel.

"And I will give them an heart to know me, that I am the LORD: and they shall be my people, and I will be their God: for they shall return unto me with their whole heart" (Jer. 24:7).

"Behold, the days come, saith the LORD, that I will make a new covenant with the house of Israel, and with the house of Judah: not according to the covenant that I made with their fathers in the day that I took them by the hand to bring them out of the land of Egypt; which my covenant they brake, although I was an husband unto them, saith the LORD: but this shall be the covenant that I will make with the house of Israel; after those days, saith the LORD, I will put my law in their inward parts, and write it in their hearts; and will be their God, and they shall be my people" (Jer. 31:31–33).

"For finding fault with them, he said, Behold, the days come, saith the Lord, when I will make a new covenant with the house of Israel and with the house of Judah" (Heb. 8:8).

Christ is the One to institute this new covenant which is yet future. Righteousness by faith is indeed witnessed to by the Law and prophets. In the meantime, it is not necessary to ascend to heaven to bring Christ down. He has already come the first time and died. It is not necessary to raise Him from the dead. He has been already raised from the dead.

They had the Law for 1500 years and they knew it as a matter of rote and ritual, but it had not brought righteousness. Christ had come to them just as the Law had come. It was not something that was far off, and Christ had come among them. He died and rose again in their midst. The "of-faith-righteousness" was available to them as it is to us because it has been preached down through the ages. The Law bore witness to both the righteousness by law and righteousness by faith. It is not "the commandments" in Deuteronomy 30, but "commandment." The "of-law-righteousness" had not brought salvation, but the "of-faith-righteousness" does bring salvation.

A careful examination of the passage in Deuteronomy 30 will reveal that Paul is not giving an exact quotation, but that he is making an application of the passage. The statement of Beet is pertinent, "This appeal to Moses is a remarkable example of skillful and correct exegesis."

> **See, I have set before thee this day life and good, and death and evil;**
>
> **In that I command thee this day to love the LORD thy God, to walk in his ways, and to keep his commandments and his statutes and his judgments, that thou mayest live and multiply: and the LORD thy God shall bless thee in the land whither thou goest to possess it [Deut. 30:15–16].**

Their stay in the land will be determined by their obedience. He outlines their history and says they will go out of that land when they disobey. But God promises to bring them back. Finally, He will return them and they shall never, never go out again. Why? Because they will obey Him? No. Because God makes good His covenant. He will bring them back, and then they will obey Him.

It is exactly the same with us. God asks us to trust the Lord Jesus Christ as our Savior. After that He talks to us about obedience—"If ye love me, keep my commandments" (John 14:15).

> **That thou mayest love the LORD thy God, and that thou mayest obey his voice, and that thou mayest cleave unto him: for he is thy life, and the length of thy days: that thou mayest dwell in the land which the LORD sware unto they fathers, to Abraham, to Isaac, and to Jacob, to give them [Deut. 30:20].**

I repeat it again: Love and obedience is the great theme of Deuteronomy. If this was so important for the children of Israel, how important it is for you and me in this day of grace when we have been given so much more light. Since we have been given more, our responsibility is greater. One of the things I pray for more devoutly than anything else is that I may be kept close to Him today. Oh, friends, we need to be kept close to the Lord Jesus Christ. How important it is!

CHAPTER 31

THEME: Moses' last counsels

We have come now to the last section of the Book of Deuteronomy. It is a requiem to Moses and extends from chapter 31 through 34. It begins with the fifth oration which Moses gave to the children of Israel and which is recorded in this book.

We are coming to the end of the life of Moses. The entire Bible up to this point has been written by Moses. A great deal of it has been about Moses. He has been a key person ever since the time they came out of the land of Egypt. He has been concerned with Israel for forty years, and he has left us a record of the 120 years of his life. Now he is getting ready to die.

And Moses went and spake these words unto all Israel.

And he said unto them, I am an hundred and twenty years old this day; I can no more go out and come in: also the Lord hath said unto me, thou shalt not go over this Jordan [Deut. 31:1–2].

Note the two statements about himself. He is getting old. We all get old, and most of us will not make it to 120. When we move toward that area, we are no longer vital as far as God's program is concerned. Moses is not the essential one to bring Israel into the Promised Land. God has made it very clear to him that a new leader will take the people over the Jordan River and into the land. Moses will not be the leader much longer.

The Lord thy God, he will go over before thee, and he will destroy these nations from before thee, and thou shalt possess them: and Joshua, he shall go over before thee, as the Lord hath said [Deut. 31:3].

Moses did not choose Joshua; *God* selected him to be the leader to succeed Moses. I doubt whether Moses would have chosen Joshua if the choice had been left to him. Actually, Caleb seems more impressive than Joshua, and it would seem more natural for him to be the new leader. Or, (after all, Moses is human) wouldn't he have been apt to choose one of his own sons to succeed him? That was the way the Pharaohs did down in Egypt, and it would be natural for Moses to do the same thing. So God chose Joshua to lead them over the Jordan. Moses is no longer essential.

That has a great lesson for us. It teaches us that none of us are essential to God's program. God uses each man in his own time, but when the time of work for the man is finished, God's work still goes on.

I can remember a pastor who was up in years telling me, "I just can't retire because I am so essential to this work." Since then he died in the harness, but the interesting thing is that the work prospered more after he died than it had before. We may think we are essential, but we are not. When the time comes for us to step aside, God will raise up someone else. That is what is happening to Moses here.

Be strong and of a good courage, fear not, nor be afraid of them: for the LORD thy God, he it is that doth go with thee; he will not fail thee, nor forsake thee [Deut. 31:6].

Moses is encouraging these people not to fear the enemy tribes that are in the land. You will notice that he encourages this generation over and over, telling them to cross over into the land. He had lived through the experience of Kadesh-barnea. He had seen the older generation turn yellow and run back into the wilderness. So Moses over and over again encourages this new generation to go on in, assuring them that God will lead them into the land.

And Moses called unto Joshua, and said unto him in the sight of all Israel, Be strong and of a good courage: for thou must go with this people unto the land which the

LORD hath sworn unto their fathers to give them: and
thou shalt cause them to inherit it [Deut. 31:7].

This was good; this is as it should be. He encourages Joshua before all
the people. By encouraging Joshua, he is also encouraging the people.

And the LORD, he it is that doth go before thee; he will be
with thee, he will not fail thee, neither forsake thee: fear
not, neither be dismayed [Deut. 31:8].

This was the same lesson that Isaiah had to learn. Remember that the
sixth chapter of Isaiah starts, "In the year that king Uzziah died I saw
also the Lord sitting upon a throne. . . ." Poor Isaiah! Uzziah had been
a good king, and now that he was dead, Isaiah thought things were
really going to be bad. Another king would be raised up and the nation would just go to the dogs, so to speak. But what did he find when
he went into the temple? He found that God was still on the throne,
that the real King of Israel and of Judah was still on the throne. He
wasn't dead. He wasn't even sick. Isaiah learned that although Uzziah
had died, God was still very much alive.

And Moses wrote this law, and delivered it unto the
priests the sons of Levi, which bare the ark of the covenant of the LORD, and unto all the elders of Israel [Deut.
31:9].

Remember that Deuteronomy began, "These are the words which
Moses spoke." There are about eight orations of Moses in the book—
given orally, then written down. Moses wrote this Law. As you may
know, the Graf-Wellhausen theory rejects the Mosiac authorship, con-
sidering the Pentateuch as historical documents compiled shortly before 400 B.C. The original argument for this theory was that writing
was not in existence at the time of Moses. Of course archaeologists
have found that writing was in existence long before Moses' day, but
the Graf-Wellhausen theory is still held by the liberal wing of the
church for the obvious reason that the prediction of Israel's declension

after entering the land is so accurate that the unbeliever would like to think it was written as history rather than prophecy.

Now even at this time, when the children of Israel are ready to enter the land, you would think that God wouldn't take them in if there were a chance of their failing. Yet He tells Moses here this is exactly what will happen. God knows human nature. He knows your being and my being. My friend, you and I would walk away from God in the next ten minutes if He didn't keep us close to Himself.

Now notice what the Lord says to Moses:

> **And the LORD said unto Moses, Behold, thy days approach that thou must die: call Joshua, and present yourselves in the tabernacle of the congregation, that I may give him a charge. And Moses and Joshua went, and presented themselves in the tabernacle of the congregation.**
>
> **And the LORD appeared in the tabernacle in a pillar of a cloud: and the pillar of the cloud stood over the door of the tabernacle.**
>
> **And the LORD said unto Moses, Behold, thou shalt sleep with thy fathers; and this people will rise up, and go a-whoring after the gods of the strangers of the land, whither they go to be among them, and will forsake me, and break my covenant which I have made with them.**
>
> **Then my anger shall be kindled against them in that day, and I will forsake them, and I will hide my face from them, and they shall be devoured, and many evils and troubles shall befall them; so that they will say in that day, Are not these evils come upon us, because our God is not among us? [Deut. 31:14–17].**

Now I know that there are people who say, "We are different today. We'll not turn away from God." But do you know that the Lord Jesus said the same thing about the church? In Luke 18:8 He said, "Nevertheless when the Son of man cometh, shall he find faith on the earth?" "Faith" is the faith, the whole body of revealed truth. The answer to that is no, He won't. In fact, the way the question is couched in the Greek demands a negative answer. In the New Testament there is predicted the apostasy of the church, just as it was predicted of Israel, and you and I are living in it today. I have seen in my day that which curdles my blood. I have watched church after church, which at one time was conservative, take the emphasis off the Word of God and finally depart from the faith. And I have seen man after man, who at one time professed to be sound in the faith, turn away from the things of God. Now don't say that you can't do it or that I can't do it. In these days I pray more than anything else, "Oh, God, keep me close to Thee."

> Now therefore write ye this song for you, and teach it the children of Israel: put it in their mouths, that this song may be witness for me against the children of Israel.
>
> For when I shall have brought them into the land which I sware unto their fathers, that floweth with milk and honey; and they shall have eaten and filled themselves, and waxen fat; then will they turn unto other gods, and serve them, and provoke me, and break my covenant.
>
> And it shall come to pass, when many evils and troubles are befallen them, that this song shall testify against them as a witness; for it shall not be forgotten out of the mouths of their seed: for I know their imagination which they go about, even now, before I have brought them into the land which I sware [Deut. 31:19–21].

Music is a very important factor. We are all greatly influenced by music. Right now some of the music that is getting into our churches is a disgrace, according to this poor preacher's opinion. Someone needs to speak out against it. The music must say something, must have a message that will draw people closer to the Lord Jesus. Too much of our music attempts to reach the modern generation all right, but fails to meet them with the gospel of Jesus Christ.

In the next chapter we will read the song. The interesting thing about the song is that it is rock music. Do I really mean that? Yes, it is all about the Rock, who is Christ. That is the kind of rock music that Moses taught to Israel, and that is the kind of rock music we need today.

> **And it came to pass, when Moses had made an end of writing the words of this law in a book, until they were finished,**
>
> **That Moses commanded the Levites, which bare the ark of the covenant of the Lord, saying,**
>
> **Take this book of the law, and put it in the side of the ark of the covenant of the Lord your God, that it may be there for a witness against thee [Deut. 31:24–26].**

This "book," you understand, was not a book such as we have today. It was a scroll or it may even have been a clay tablet. However, in Moses' day they had scrolls and this law was probably written on a scroll.

Remember that we are in the section which we have labeled the requiem of Moses. He is getting into his final report to the nation. He calls the tribes around him just as old Jacob had called the twelve sons around him. The twelve sons have now become the twelve tribes, and they are a great nation. Moses calls them to him.

> **For I know thy rebellion, and thy stiff neck: behold, while I am yet alive with you this day, ye have been rebellious against the Lord; and how much more after my death?**
>
> **Gather unto me all the elders of your tribes, and your officers, that I may speak these words in their ears, and call heaven and earth to record against them.**

> For I know that after my death ye will utterly corrupt yourselves, and turn aside from the way which I have commanded you; and evil will befall you in the latter days; because ye will do evil in the sight of the LORD, to provoke him to anger through the work of your hands.
>
> And Moses spake in the ears of all the congregation of Israel the words of this song, until they were ended [Deut. 31:27–30].

May I say that this statement which Moses made about 3500 years ago is still accurate, still true. It has been fulfilled quite literally. It is also true of the entire human family, for God has said that mankind apart from God will utterly corrupt itself. All we need to do is look around us today and we can see that this is true.

CHAPTER 32

THEME: Moses' final song

The Song of Moses is a great song, in fact, a magnificent song in many ways. The nation of Israel was to learn it. It was to be somewhat like their national anthem. It was a song given to them by God; every Israelite was to learn it and teach it to his children.

As I indicated before, music is a very important factor in the life of a nation. Someone has said, "Let me write the music of a nation, and I do not care who writes the laws." In other words, the songs have more influence than do the laws! If this is true, we today are in a sad predicament. Modern music has sunk to a level that is absolutely frightening.

The first four verses of the Song of Moses are the introduction.

Give ear, O ye heavens, and I will speak; and hear, O earth, the words of my mouth [Deut. 32:1].

God calls heaven and earth to witness that these are the conditions under which He is putting Israel into the land. When He is ready to put Israel out of the land in judgment, Israel records this same call. In fact, that is the way the Book of Isaiah opens: "The vision of Isaiah the son of Amoz, which he saw concerning Judah and Jerusalem in the days of Uzziah, Jotham, Ahaz, and Hezekiah, kings of Judah. Hear, O heavens, and give ear, O earth: for the LORD hath spoken, I have nourished and brought up children, and they have rebelled against me" (Isa. 1:1–2). When God put Israel into the land, He called heaven and earth to witness. When God is ready to put them out of the land, about seven hundred years later, He again calls heaven and earth to witness. God is not doing this in a corner; this is not something which He does under cover. He is justified in putting them out of the land.

My doctrine shall drop as the rain, my speech shall distil as the dew, as the small rain upon the tender herb, and as the showers upon the grass [Deut. 32:2].

That is the way the Word of God is. The psalmist says, "He shall come down like rain upon the mown grass: as showers that water the earth" (Ps. 72:6). I love that statement. A dear saint in Dallas, Texas, lost her husband whom she loved dearly. She told her pastor that now she understood the meaning of that verse in the Psalms. She was the mown grass, but God came to her through His Word like the gentle rain. That is the way the Word of God should come down in our lives. Here in Southern California, we go through an entire summer without rain. Normally, in the fall we have quite a rain that begins the autumn season. The earth just opens up to receive it. It washes the leaves on the trees, and everything becomes clean and sharply clear. God desires that the Word of God should come down into our hearts and lives like this.

> **Because I will publish the name of the LORD: ascribe ye greatness unto our God [Deut. 32:3].**

How little of our literature today promotes God or has anything good to say about Him! Usually His name is taken in vain if it is used at all.

> **He is the Rock, his work is perfect: for all his ways are judgment: a God of truth and without iniquity, just and right is he [Deut. 32:4].**

This is the song about the Rock, you see. The word "Rock" is used about seven times in the song. The Lord Jesus Christ is called the Rock. Christ is the chief Cornerstone of 1 Peter 2:6. His work is perfect. Oh, how this song exalts God, and He needs to be exalted by us today.

> **They have corrupted themselves, their spot is not the spot of his children: they are a perverse and crooked generation.**

> Do ye thus requite the LORD, O foolish people and un-
> wise? is not he thy father that hath bought thee? hath he
> not made thee, and established thee? [Deut. 32:5-6].

God is the Father of Israel because of creation—He doesn't mention redemption here. In one sense God is the Father of all mankind because He created all mankind. When God created Adam he was called a son of God, but Adam sinned. After that, none of the offspring of Adam are called the sons of God unless they have become sons of God by faith in Jesus Christ. The whole human family may be pictured as a crooked generation, a foolish people.

Now we have a wonderful stanza on the goodness of God—verses 7-14.

> Remember the days of old, consider the years of many
> generations: ask thy father, and he will shew thee; thy
> elders, and they will tell thee.
>
> When the Most High divided to the nations their inheri-
> tance, when he separated the sons of Adam, he set the
> bounds of the people according to the number of the
> children of Israel.
>
> For the LORD's portion is his people; Jacob is the lot of his
> inheritance [Deut. 32:7-9].

Verse 8 is most unusual. I have never yet heard a satisfactory explanation of it. The nations of the earth are measured according to the number of the children of Israel. In other words, the bounds that the nations have are arranged according to the number of Israelites. This is something that needs a great deal of study today. It explains why the Jew and his land are the most sensitive areas on the earth.

> He found him in a desert land, and in the waste howling
> wilderness; he led him about, he instructed him, he
> kept him as the apple of his eye [Deut. 32:10].

For forty years in that howling wilderness, that great and terrible wilderness, God led His people and kept them. Why? They were the apple of His eye—a lovely expression.

Now we have one of the great statements in Scripture:

As an eagle stirreth up her nest, fluttereth over her young, spreadeth abroad her wings, taketh them, beareth them on her wings:

So the Lord alone did lead him, and there was no strange god with him [Deut. 32:11–12].

At the time when the little eaglets ought to be out spreading their wings, they are perfectly willing to stay in the nest and let mama and papa bring them food all day long, then take care of them at night. The day comes when the mother eagle pushes those little ones off the cliff, and they have to stretch those wings. But suppose a little eaglet does not do very well. That mother, with those tremendous wings of hers, comes right up under the little eaglet, catches him on her wings, then lifts him back up to the rock and gives him a few more worms to eat for the next few days. Then she tries him out again. This is the way God watches over those who are His own. God pushes us out of the nest sometimes, not because He doesn't love us but because He wants us to learn to fly—He wants us to learn to live for Him.

This is a wonderful description of the goodness of Jehovah.

But Jeshurun waxed fat, and kicked: thou art waxen fat, thou art grown thick, thou art covered with fatness; then he forsook God which made him, and lightly esteemed the Rock of his salvation [Deut. 32:15].

"Jeshurun" is another name for Israel. Israel waxed fat, and kicked! What a picture this is of the affluent society we have in America today. And what a bunch of complainers there are—and the Christians join with them. "Thou art waxed fat, thou art grown thick" means these folk were getting fat. In their prosperity, they didn't think their Rock was important anymore.

> They provoked him to jealousy with strange gods, with abominations provoked they him to anger.
>
> They sacrificed unto devils, not to God; to gods whom they knew not, to new gods that came newly up, whom your fathers feared not.
>
> Of the Rock that begat thee thou art unmindful, and hast forgotten God that formed thee [Deut. 32:16-18].

In this next section (vv. 19-25) we see the judgment of God upon His people.

> And when the Lord saw it, he abhorred them, because of the provoking of his sons, and of his daughters.
>
> And he said, I will hide my face from them, I will see what their end shall be: for they are a very froward generation, children in whom is no faith [Deut. 32:19-20].

God says that He will hide Himself from them. He will not manifest Himself to them.

The next section, verses 26-42, expresses God's longing for His people.

> I said, I would scatter them into corners, I would make the remembrance of them to cease from among men:
>
> Were it not that I feared the wrath of the enemy, lest their adversaries should behave themselves strangely, and

**lest they should say, Our hand is high, and the LORD
hath not done all this [Deut. 32:26-27].**

God says He would scatter Israel into corners, were it not that He
feared for them the wrath of the enemy. He says, "I don't want them to
hurt My people or destroy them, 'Lest their adversaries should behave
themselves strangely, and lest they should say, Our hand is high, and
the LORD hath not done all this.'"

**For they are a nation void of counsel, neither is there any
understanding in them.**

**O that they were wise, that they understood this, that
they would consider their latter end!**

**How should one chase a thousand, and two put ten thou-
sand to flight, except their Rock had sold them, and the
LORD had shut them up?**

**For their rock is not as our Rock, even our enemies
themselves being judges [Deut. 32:28-31].**

What a picture we have here! God has a longing for His people. He
wants to redeem them. He wants to save them.

Now we come to the final stanza of the song: the nations of the
world will be blessed with Israel.

**Rejoice, O ye nations, with his people: for he will avenge
the blood of his servants, and will render vengeance to
his adversaries, and will be merciful unto his land, and
to his people [Deut. 32:43].**

This concludes this magnificent Song of Moses.

**And Moses came and spake all the words of this song in
the ears of the people, he, and Hoshea the son of Nun
[Deut. 32:44].**

"Hoshea" is Joshua, by the way.

> And Moses made an end of speaking all these words to all Israel [Deut. 32:45].

THE FINAL EXHORTATION

> And he said unto them, Set your hearts unto all the words which I testify among you this day, which ye shall command your children to observe to do, all the words of this law.

> For it is not a vain thing for you; because it is your life: and through this thing ye shall prolong your days in the land, whither ye go over Jordan to possess it [Deut. 32:46–47].

Again, their tenure in the land would depend on their obedience.

> And the LORD spake unto Moses that selfsame day, saying,

> Get thee up into this mountain Abarim, unto mount Nebo, which is the land of Moab, that is over against Jericho; and behold the land of Canaan, which I give unto the children of Israel for a possession:

> And die in the mount whither thou goest up, and be gathered unto thy people; as Aaron thy brother died in mount Hor, and was gathered unto his people:

> Because ye trespassed against me among the children of Israel at the waters of Meribah-Kadesh, in the wilderness of Zin; because ye sanctified me not in the midst of the children of Israel.

> Yet thou shalt see the land before thee; but thou shalt not go thither unto the land which I give the children of Israel [Deut. 32:48–52].

Moses, the representative of the Law, the lawgiver, cannot enter into the land. Legalism is actually a hindrance. The Law is a *revealer,* not a remover of sin. The Law cannot save. The Law could not bring Moses into the land. Neither can the Law bring us into the place of blessing.

CHAPTER 33

THEME: Moses' final blessing of the tribes

The last public act of Moses before his death is to gather his people about him by tribes and give a blessing to each one.

> **And this is the blessing, wherewith Moses the man of God blessed the children of Israel before his death [Deut. 33:1].**

He begins with Reuben.

> **Let Reuben live, and not die; and let not his men be few [Deut. 33:6].**

Moses prays that Reuben will never become extinct as a tribe in Israel.

> **And this is the blessing of Judah: and he said, Hear LORD, the voice of Judah, and bring him unto his people: let his hands be sufficient for him; and be thou an help to him from his enemies [Deut. 33:7].**

Judah is the royal tribe from which the Messiah is to come.

> **And of Levi he said, Let thy Thummim and thy Urim be with thy only one, whom thou didst prove at Massah, and with whom thou didst strive at the waters of Meribah;**

> They shall teach Jacob thy judgments, and Israel thy
> law: they shall put incense before thee, and whole burnt
> sacrifice upon thine altar.
>
> Bless, LORD, his substance, and accept the work of his
> hands: smite through the loins of them that rise against
> him, and of them that hate him, that they rise not again
> [Deut. 33:8, 10–11].

This tribe was honored by the priesthood in the family of Aaron. They had the privilege of teaching the Law. The nation will be blessed through Levi.

Blessing is to come to Israel through the tribes of Joseph, which are Ephraim and Manasseh.

An interesting blessing is in verse 24.

> And of Asher he said, Let Asher be blessed with chil-
> dren; let him be acceptable to his brethren, and let him
> dip his foot in oil [Deut. 33:24].

It is interesting that years ago a pipeline of oil came into the northern part of the kingdom through the land of Asher. It may be that that pipeline will be opened.

> There is none like unto the God of Jeshurun, who rideth
> upon the heaven in thy help, and in his excellency on the
> sky.
>
> The eternal God is thy refuge, and underneath are the
> everlasting arms: and he shall thrust out the enemy
> from before thee; and shall say, Destroy them.
>
> Israel then shall dwell in safety alone: the fountain of
> Jacob shall be upon a land of corn and wine; also his
> heavens shall drop down dew.

Happy art thou, O Israel: who is like unto thee, O people saved by the LORD, the shield of thy help, and who is the sword of thy excellency! and thine enemies shall be found liars unto thee; and thou shalt tread upon their high places [Deut. 33:26–29].

Oh, if only Israel had obeyed God!

CHAPTER 34

THEME: The death of Moses

The question arises whether Moses wrote of his own death. He could have. The Lord had told him he would die. I have had funeral services for individuals who wrote out the details of the entire service before they died. However, a great many believe that this is part of the Book of Joshua. This certainly may be, since originally there were not the book divisions that we have today. The Old Testament was written on scrolls with one book following another. Therefore, this may actually be the beginning of the Book of Joshua.

And Moses went up from the plains of Moab unto the mountain of Nebo, to the top of Pisgah, that is over against Jericho. And the LORD shewed him all the land of Gilead, unto Dan.

And all Naphtali, and the land of Ephraim, and Manasseh, and all the land of Judah, unto the utmost sea.

And the south, and the plain of the valley of Jericho, the city of palm trees, unto Zoar.

And the LORD said unto him, This is the land which I sware unto Abraham, unto Isaac, and unto Jacob, saying, I will give it unto thy seed: I have caused thee to see it with thine eyes, but thou shalt not go over thither.

So Moses the servant of the LORD died there in the land of Moab, according to the word of the LORD.

And he buried him in a valley in the land of Moab, over

against Beth-peor: but no man knoweth of his sepulchre unto this day [Deut. 34:1–6].

Why was his sepulchre unknown? Because of the fact that Moses was to be raised from the dead and brought into the Promised Land. You will remember that when the Lord Jesus was transfigured on the mount, both Moses and Elijah appeared with Him and spoke about His approaching death. So, you see, Moses did get to the Promised Land eventually. The Law could not bring Moses into the land, but the Lord Jesus Christ brought him in.

And Moses was an hundred and twenty years old when he died: his eye was not dim, nor his natural force abated.

And the children of Israel wept for Moses in the plains of Moab thirty days: so the days of weeping and mourning for Moses were ended [Deut. 34:7–8].

> By Nebo's lonely mountain,
>   On this side Jordan's wave,
> In a vale in the land of Moab,
>   There lies a lonely grave.
>
> And no man knows that sepulchre,
>   And no man saw it e'er,
> For the angels of God upturned the sod,
>   And laid the dead man there.
>   —Cecil Francis Alexander
>   "The Burial of Moses"

Again, why was his grave kept secret? Well, after all, Satan would not want Moses to appear on the Mount of Transfiguration. God took care of this by performing the burial of Moses Himself.

Although to us it may seem like a lonely death, one translation has it, "He died by the kiss of God." It is a lovely thought that God just kissed Moses and put him to sleep. What a picture we have here!

It is with a note of sadness that we close the Book of Deuteronomy, but we will be going with the children of Israel into the Land of Promise in the Book of Joshua.

BIBLIOGRAPHY
(Recommended for Further Study)

Epp, Theodore H. *Moses*. Lincoln, Nebraska: Back to the Bible Broadcast, 1975.

Gaebelein, Arno C. *Annotated Bible*. Vol. 1. Neptune, New Jersey: Loizeaux Brothers, n.d.

Grant, F. W. *Numerical Bible*. Neptune, New Jersey: Loizeaux Brothers, 1891.

Gray, James M. *Synthetic Bible Studies*. Old Tappan, New Jersey: Fleming H. Revell Co., 1906.

Jensen, Irving L. *Numbers & Deuteronomy—Self Study Guide*. Chicago, Illinois: Moody Press, 1967.

Kelly, William. *Lectures Introductory to the Pentateuch*. Oak Park, Illinois: Bible Truth Publishers, 1870.

Mackintosh, C. H. (C.H.M.). *Notes on the Pentateuch*. Neptune, New Jersey: Loizeaux Brothers, 1880.

Meyer, F. B. *Moses: The Servant of God*. Fort Washington, Pennsylvania: Christian Literature Crusade, n.d.

Ridderbos, J. *Deuteronomy*. Grand Rapids, Michigan: Zondervan Publishing House, 1984.

Schultz, Samuel J. *Deuteronomy: The Gospel of Love*. Chicago, Illinois: Moody Press, 1971.

Schneider, Bernard N. *Deuteronomy*. Winona Lake, Indiana: Brethren Missionary Herald Co.

Thomas, W. H. Griffith. *Through the Pentateuch Chapter by Chapter*. Grand Rapids, Michigan: William B. Eerdmans Publishing Co., 1957.

Unger, Merrill F. *Unger's Bible Handbook*. Chicago, Illinois: Moody Press, 1966.

Unger, Merrill F. *Unger's Commentary on the Old Testament*. Vol. I. Chicago, Illinois: Moody Press, 1981.